I0426423

June 2012

SUPPLEMENTAL SECURITY INCOME

Better Management Oversight Needed for Children's Benefits

G A O
Accountability * Integrity * Reliability

GAO
Accountability * Integrity * Reliability

Highlights

Highlights of GAO-12-497, a report to congressional requesters

SUPPLEMENTAL SECURITY INCOME

Better Management Oversight Needed for Children's Benefits

Why GAO Did This Study

SSA's SSI program provides cash benefits to eligible low-income individuals with disabilities, including children. In 2011, SSA paid more than $9 billion to about 1.3 million disabled children, the majority of whom received benefits due to a mental impairment. GAO was asked to assess (1) trends in the rate of children receiving SSI benefits due to mental impairments over the past decade; (2) the role that medical and nonmedical information, such as medication and school records, play in the initial determination of a child's eligibility; and (3) steps SSA has taken to monitor the continued medical eligibility of these children.

To do this, GAO analyzed program data; interviewed SSA officials; conducted site visits to 9 field offices and 11 state DDS offices across the nation; reviewed a generalizable sample of 298 claims for select impairments from fiscal year 2010; reviewed relevant federal laws and regulations; and interviewed external experts, among others.

What GAO Recommends

GAO recommends that SSA take steps to ensure needed information, such as secondary impairment data and school records, is consistently collected; make its CDR waiver process more transparent; and conduct additional childhood CDRs. SSA agreed with four recommendations and disagreed with one that the agency conduct additional childhood CDRs, citing resource constraints. The GAO recommendation acknowledges resource constraints, as discussed more fully within the report.

View GAO-12-497. To view the e-supplement online, click on GAO-12-498SP. For more information, contact Daniel Bertoni at (202) 512-7215 or bertonid@gao.gov.

What GAO Found

The number of Supplemental Security Income (SSI) child applicants and recipients with mental impairments has increased substantially for more than a decade, even though the Social Security Administration (SSA) denied, on average, 54 percent of such claims from fiscal years 2000 to 2011. Factors such as the rising number of children in poverty and increasing diagnosis of certain mental impairments have likely contributed to this growth. In fiscal year 2011, the most prevalent primary mental impairments among children found medically eligible were (1) attention deficit hyperactivity disorder, (2) speech and language delay, and (3) autism, with autism claims growing most rapidly since fiscal year 2000. State disability determination services (DDS) examiners also consider the impact of additional, or "secondary," impairments when making a decision, and when present, these impairments were used to support 55 percent of those cases GAO reviewed that were allowed in fiscal year 2010. However, SSA has not consistently collected those impairment data, limiting its understanding of how all impairments may affect decisions.

DDS examiners generally rely on a combination of key medical and nonmedical information—such as medical records and teacher assessments—to determine a child's medical eligibility for SSI. In its case file review, GAO found that examiners usually cited four to five information sources as the basis for their decision, and that being on medication was never the sole source of support for decisions. Moreover, examiners cited medication and treatment information, such as reports of improved functioning, as a basis for denying benefits in more than half of cases that GAO reviewed, despite a perception among some parents that medicating their child would result in an award of benefits. Examiners also reported they sometimes lacked complete information to inform their decision making. For example, several DDS offices reported obstacles to obtaining information from schools, which they believe to be critical in understanding how a child functions. Examiners also do not routinely receive information from SSA field offices on multiple children who receive benefits in the same household, which SSA's fraud investigations unit has noted as an indicator of possible fraud or abuse. Without such information, examiners may be limited in their ability to identify threats to program integrity.

SSA has conducted fewer continuing disability reviews (CDR) for children since 2000, even though it is generally required by law to review the medical eligibility of certain children at least every 3 years. From fiscal year 2000 to 2011, childhood CDRs overall fell from more than 150,000 to about 45,000 (a 70 percent decrease), while CDRs for children with mental impairments dropped from more than 84,000 to about 16,000 (an 80 percent decrease). The most recent data show that more than 400,000 CDRs were overdue for children with mental impairments, with some pending by as many as 13 years or more. Of the more than 24,000 CDRs found to be 6 or more years overdue, 25 percent were for children expected to medically improve within 6 to 18 months of their initial allowance. SSA acknowledged the importance of conducting such reviews, but said that due to resource constraints and other workloads, such as initial claims, most childhood CDRs are a lower priority. SSA's process for issuing waivers from the CDR legal requirement lacks transparency, and without these reviews, SSA could continue to forgo significant program savings.

United States Government Accountability Office

Contents

Figures

Abbreviations

ADHD	attention deficit hyperactivity disorder
CHIP	Children's Health Insurance Program
CDR	continuing disability review
DDS	disability determination services
IDEA	Individuals with Disabilities Education Act
PRWORA	Personal Responsibility and Work Opportunity Reconciliation Act of 1996
SSA	Social Security Administration
SSDI	Social Security Disability Insurance
SSI	Supplemental Security Income

View GAO-12-497 Key Component

- Supplemental Security Income: State Trends in Applications, Allowances, and Benefit Receipts for Children with Mental Impairments (GAO-12-498SP, June 2012), and E-supplement to GAO-12-497

United States Government Accountability Office
Washington, DC 20548

June 26, 2012

The Honorable Susan Collins
Ranking Member
Committee on Homeland Security and Government Affairs
United States Senate

The Honorable Thomas R. Carper
Chairman
The Honorable Scott Brown
Ranking Member
Subcommittee on Federal Financial Management, Government
Information, Federal Services, and International Security
Committee on Homeland Security and Government Affairs
United States Senate

The Honorable Geoff Davis
Chairman
Subcommittee on Human Resources
Committee on Ways and Means
House of Representatives

The Honorable Richard E. Neal
House of Representatives

The Social Security Administration (SSA) administers the Supplemental
Security Income (SSI) program, a nationwide federal assistance program
that provides cash benefits to eligible low-income individuals with
disabilities, including children, as well as certain individuals who are aged
or blind. In 2011, SSA paid almost $50 billion in SSI benefits to about 8
million recipients, of which about $9.4 billion was paid to 1.3 million
children. During the early and mid-1990s, the SSI program grew at an
unprecedented rate for children due, in part, to legal developments that
expanded program eligibility for children with mental impairments. For
example, from the end of 1989 through 1996, the number of children
receiving SSI benefits more than tripled from 265,000 to about 955,000.
Since that time, the overall number of children receiving SSI benefits has
continued to rise. In addition to this growth, the media has suggested that
many parents believe it is necessary that their child be prescribed
psychotropic drugs in order to qualify for benefits.

In light of these developments, you asked us to assess, in part, the extent to which SSA is monitoring the initial determination and continued eligibility of children with mental impairments. Specifically, this report addresses (1) the trends in the rate of children receiving SSI benefits due to mental impairments over the past decade; (2) the role that medical and nonmedical information, such as medication and school records, play in the initial determination of a child's eligibility; and (3) the steps SSA has taken to monitor the continued medical eligibility of these children.

To examine these issues, we analyzed SSA data on trends and characteristics of children applying for and receiving SSI benefits. We assessed the reliability of the data presented in this report by performing data testing, reviewing internal controls and related documentation, and interviewing agency officials, and found potential limitations with the extent to which primary and secondary impairment coding may be present within SSA's 831 Disability file—the computer file that contains data on disability determinations. However, because SSA uses the 831 Disability file to make (and thus, reflect) the decisions regarding medical determinations, we determined that these data were sufficiently reliable to describe certain trends among children in the SSI program. To corroborate these data and better understand what information sources examiners use in determining a child's medical eligibility, we reviewed a generalizable probability sample of 298 SSI cases[1] from the 184,150 initial determinations performed in fiscal year 2010 for children with alleged attention deficit hyperactivity disorder (ADHD),[2] speech and language delay, and autistic disorder and other pervasive development disorders (autism).[3] We also conducted in-depth interviews with SSA management and line staff at SSA headquarters and within six SSA regions. These regions are Atlanta, Georgia; Dallas, Texas; Chicago,

---

[1]We originally sampled 300 cases for review but encountered 2 cases that were either mis-coded or that lacked an electronic case file. We excluded these 2 cases from our analysis, which produced an effective sample size of 298.

[2]Children with attention deficit disorder are also included in this category.

[3]These were the most prevalent primary mental impairments among those children found medically eligible in fiscal year 2011. Percentage estimates for initial determinations of children with alleged ADHD, speech and language delay, and autism are based on the sample and are subject to sampling error. Unless otherwise noted, we are 95 percent confident that our estimates are within plus or minus 8 percentage points of what we would have obtained if we had reviewed cases for the entire population. Appendix I provides more information about the design of our sample.

Illinois; Philadelphia, Pennsylvania; Boston, Massachusetts; and San Francisco, California. Our work included site visits to 9 field offices within these regions, as well as 11 state disability determination services (DDS) offices (state agencies under the direction of SSA that perform medical eligibility determinations and continuing disability reviews of SSI applicants). We selected these sites on the basis of (1) their geographic location, (2) high volume of SSI applications for children with mental impairments, and (3) benefit allowance rates for children with mental impairments. In addition, we interviewed numerous external experts from the medical and disability advocacy communities and reviewed relevant studies, as well as relevant federal laws and regulations.

We conducted this performance audit from February 2011 to June 2012 in accordance with generally accepted government auditing standards. Those standards require that we plan and perform the audit to obtain sufficient, appropriate evidence to provide a reasonable basis for our findings and conclusions based on our audit objectives. We believe the evidence obtained provides a reasonable basis for findings and conclusions based on our audit objectives. Appendix I discusses our scope and methodology in further detail.

Background

Eligibility Criteria

Since 1974, the SSI program, under Title XVI of the Social Security Act, as amended,[4] has provided benefits to low-income blind and disabled persons—including adults and children,[5] as well as certain aged individuals—who meet financial eligibility requirements and the definition of disability. For individuals under age 18, a disability is a medically determinable physical or mental impairment that results in marked and severe functional limitations, and is expected to result in death or which

---

[4]The SSI program was established by Pub. L. No. 92-603, § 301, 86 Stat. 1329, 1465 (1972), and became effective starting in 1974.

[5]For purposes of the SSI program, the term "child" means an individual who is neither married nor (as determined by the Commissioner of Social Security) the head of a household, and who is (1) under the age of 18, or (2) under the age of 22 and (as determined by the Commissioner of Social Security) a student regularly attending a school, college, or university, or a course of vocational or technical training designed to prepare him or her for gainful employment. 42 U.S.C. § 1382c(c).

GAO-12-497 Supplemental Security Income

has lasted or can be expected to last for a continuous period of at least 12 months.[6] Families of children receiving SSI payments are generally required to use the benefit to meet a child's needs, including food, clothing, and shelter.[7] The maximum federal benefit payment for a child receiving SSI benefits in 2012 is $698 per month, regardless of the severity of the child's impairment.[8] As of December 2011, the average monthly federal child payment was $592.

To apply for benefits, the child's parent or guardian usually submits an application to SSA either in person at a local SSA office, by telephone, or by mail. SSA's field offices are responsible for initially processing these applications and for verifying the child's and legal guardian's nonmedical eligibility requirements, including income, resources, and living arrangement information. After initial verification, the field office transmits the case file to their state disability determination services office for a medical evaluation.[9] The medical evaluation assesses whether the child has a physical or mental impairment, or both, that (1) is severe,[10] (2) meets or medically or functionally equals impairments that are included in SSA's listing of impairments, and (3) meets the duration requirement. If these requirements are met, the child is found to be disabled for purposes of SSI.[11] The listing of impairments for children describes the impairments that cause marked and severe functional limitations.[12] If a child has a

---

[6]42 U.S.C. § 1382c(a)(3)(C)(i) and 20 C.F.R. § 416.906.

[7]Typically, a disabled child's SSI benefit is paid on behalf of the child to a "representative payee," such as a parent or guardian. The "representative payee" is responsible for using benefits received only for the child's use and benefit in a manner and for the purposes he or she determines, consistent with SSA guidelines, to be in the child's best interests. 20 C.F.R. § 416.635(a).

[8]All but five states and the Commonwealth of the Northern Mariana Islands supplement federal SSI benefits with additional payments. Fourteen states and the District of Columbia have state supplements that are either partially or wholly administered by SSA, and 31 states self administer their supplements.

[9]The medical evaluation is conducted under applicable legal requirements and SSA policy.

[10]To be considered severe, the child's impairment must cause the child more than minimal functional limitations. 20 C.F.R. § 416.924(c).

[11]20 C.F.R. § 416.924(a).

[12]See appendix II for additional information about the listings of mental disorders for children.

GAO-12-497 Supplemental Security Income

severe impairment that does not meet or medically equal any listing, the DDS will then determine whether the impairment results in limitations that functionally equal the listings.

Initial Determinations and Continuing Disability Reviews

To aid in evaluating whether a child is medically eligible, DDS offices review various medical and nonmedical information about the child, such as physician notes, psychological tests, school records, and teacher assessments.[13] In certain situations, such as when the evidence is not sufficient to support a decision as to whether a child is disabled, the DDS may purchase a consultative examination to assist in making the decision.[14] If there is evidence that indicates the existence of a mental impairment, the DDS is supposed to make every reasonable effort to ensure that a qualified psychiatrist or psychologist has completed the medical portion of the case review.[15]

After the initial determination has been made and before returning the case file to complete any outstanding nondisability case development, SSA selects a sample of initial determinations for a quality assurance review. If the case is sampled, the reviewing component sends the case to the servicing field office upon completion of its review. If the claimant is determined to be disabled, the field office computes the benefit amount and initiates benefit payment. If the claim is denied, a claimant has 60 days to request that the DDS reconsider its decision. If the claimant is dissatisfied with the reconsideration, he or she may request a hearing before an administrative law judge, whose decision may then be reviewed by SSA's Appeals Council. When these administrative review options have been exhausted, the claimant may request judicial review by filing an action in a federal district court.[16]

If SSA determines that an individual is disabled, the agency is required by law to conduct periodic reviews, known as continuing disability reviews

---

[13]20 C.F.R. § 416.913.

[14]20 C.F.R. § 416.919a(b). A consultative examination is a physical or mental examination or test purchased from a treating source or another medical source, including a pediatrician, for an individual at SSA's request and expense. 20 C.F.R. § 416.919.

[15]20 C.F.R. § 416.903(e).

[16]For more information about the administrative review process for disability determinations, see 20 C.F.R. § 416.1400 et seq.

(CDR), to verify the recipient's continued medical eligibility for receiving benefits in certain circumstances.[17] More specifically, SSA is generally required to perform CDRs (1) during the first year after birth for babies whose low birth weight is a contributing factor to the determination of disability[18] and (2) at least once every 3 years for all other children under age 18 whose conditions are considered likely to improve.[19] DDS offices determine when recipients will be due for CDRs on the basis of their potential for medical improvement, and select and schedule a review date—otherwise known as a "diary date"—for each recipient's CDR. At the time of these reviews, the child's representative payee generally must present evidence that the child is and has been receiving medically necessary and available treatment for his or her impairment. SSA is also generally required to redetermine the eligibility of children against the adult criteria[20] for disability after they reach age 18.[21]

Policy Changes to Eligibility Criteria

Since SSI's inception, a number of policy changes have influenced how SSA makes disability decisions and the extent children with mental impairments are eligible to participate in the program. In 1984, Congress mandated the development of new disability standards for individuals with mental impairments and the consideration of the impact of multiple impairments in determining disability, among other things.[22] SSA subsequently expanded the list of mental impairments it considers disabling in 1985 and again in 1990, when SSA added impairments such as ADHD.[23] In 1990, the U.S. Supreme Court decided in *Sullivan v.*

---

[17]SSA conducts two types of reviews to ensure that participants are eligible for benefits— CDRs and redeterminations. CDRs verify claimants' medical eligibility, while SSI redeterminations generally verify their financial eligibility and ensure that the recipient is receiving the right amount of SSI benefits. 20 C.F.R. §§ 416.989 and 416.204. However, age 18 redeterminations also verify claimants' medical eligibility under the adult disability criteria.

[18]42 U.S.C. § 1382c(a)(3)(H)(iv).

[19]42 U.S.C. § 1382c(a)(3)(H)(ii)(I).

[20]Adults are considered disabled if they are unable to engage in substantial gainful activity by reason of a medically determinable physical or mental impairment expected to result in death or last at least 12 months. 42 U.S.C. § 1382c(a)(3)(A).

[21]42 U.S.C. § 1382c(a)(3)(H)(iii).

[22]Pub. L. No. 98-460, §§ 4 and 5, 98 Stat. 1794, 1800, 1801.

[23]SSA maintains a list of impairments that are severe enough to be considered disabling.

Zebley that SSA's use of medical listings of impairments for children—without conducting a functional analysis—was incomplete.[24] In response, SSA established "functional equivalence" as a basis for SSI eligibility for children, whereby a child can be found medically eligible for benefits if the child's impairment limits his or her functional ability to the same degree as described in a listed impairment. In deciding whether an impairment functionally equals the listings, SSA examines how the child functions compared to children of the same age who do not have impairments—rather than basing the decision on the child's medical diagnosis. The Court's decision also resulted in the introduction of the individualized functional assessment. This assessment was intended to be comparable to SSA's method for evaluating adult impairments and to broaden the evaluation of disability in children with physical and mental impairments to include the effects of impairments on a child's ability to perform age-appropriate activities on a day-to-day basis. Awards to children, especially those with mental impairments, increased dramatically for several years following the *Sullivan v. Zebley* decision due partly to SSA readjudicating nearly 300,000 determinations made between January 1980 and February 1991 under the revised disability criteria. By 1994, SSA had reprocessed the majority of these cases, and subsequently returned to processing their normal case loads. The Personal Responsibility and Work Opportunity Reconciliation Act of 1996 (PRWORA)[25] changed the standard for children, and the act was expected to reduce the number of awards. However, awards to children with mental impairments began to increase again shortly after the legislation was enacted (see fig. 1).

---

[24]493 U.S. 521, 538-41.

[25]Pub. L. No. 104-193, 110 Stat. 2105.

Figure 1: SSI Benefit Awards to Children with Mental Impairments and Key Policy Changes, 1983 to 2011

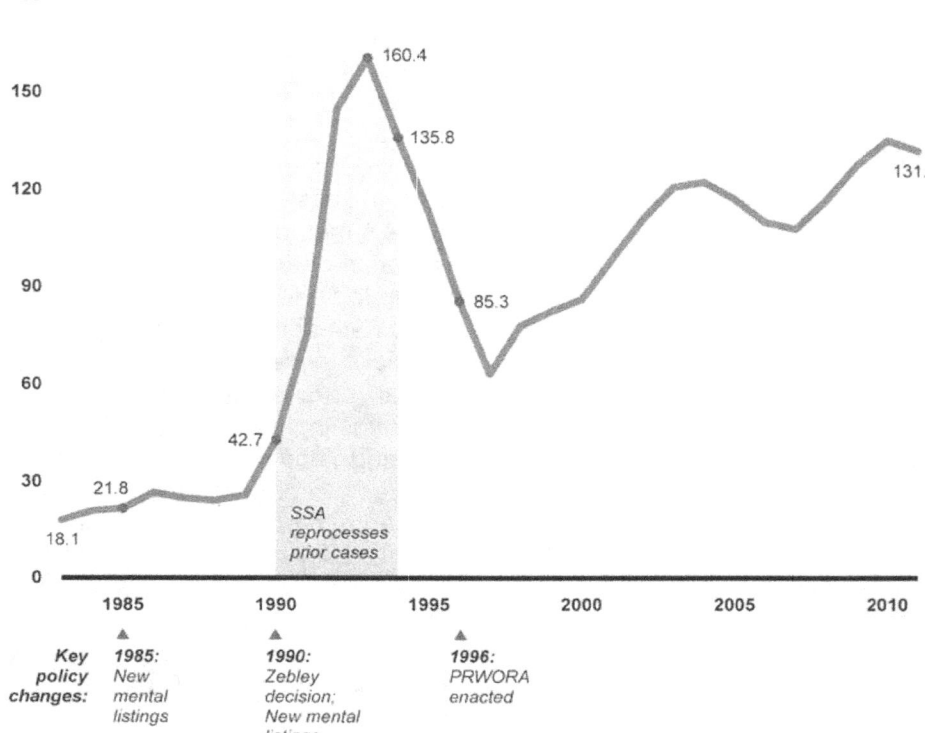

Number of children awarded benefits (in thousands)

Source: GAO analysis of SSA data from the Supplemental Security Record.

Note: Due to limited diagnosis codes available prior to 1983, SSA trend data specific to children with mental impairments are only available from 1983 to present. This figure is not intended to depict all of the possible factors which may have contributed to program trends. It is not possible to measure definitively the contribution each policy change made to these trends, and correlation does not imply causality.

Number of Children Applying for and Receiving SSI Benefits Due to Mental Impairments Has Increased

The number of children applying for and receiving SSI benefits due to a mental impairment has increased for more than a decade, and these children comprise a growing majority of all child recipients on the SSI disability rolls. While not all such children who are deemed medically eligible ultimately meet SSI's financial eligibility requirements,[26] the numbers of children applying for SSI benefits due to a mental impairment increased from 187,052 in fiscal year 2000 to 315,832 in fiscal year 2011 (a 69 percent increase).[27] Despite this increase, SSA data indicated that the agency has denied a majority of these child applicants each year. In fact, for initial determinations in fiscal years 2000 to 2011, the average denial rates for children with physical and mental impairments were about 63 and 54 percent, respectively, and allowance rates have remained relatively stable over time for both groups of children.[28] SSA data also showed that since fiscal year 2000, children with mental impairments represented the majority of all child applications and allowances for SSI benefits (see fig. 2).

---

[26]A child may be found medically eligible for benefits due to a physical or mental impairment, but SSA must verify the child's financial and other nonmedical eligibility. If these other criteria are not met, the child will not receive SSI benefits. Although the field office performs an initial verification of the child's financial eligibility prior to sending a case to the DDS office, the field office may identify additional income or assets after the DDS office completes its determination of medical eligibility.

[27]For purposes of this report, data represented as "applying" or "applications" reflect SSI benefit claims where a DDS examiner made an initial disability determination decision. Some benefit claim applications could have more than one determination if the claim is selected for a quality review or if the disability claim is updated during the same year.

[28]Data on allowances and allowance rates refers to initial level allowances, not final allowances, which include appeals decisions.

Figure 2: SSI Applications and Initial Level Allowances for Children under Age 18, by Physical and Mental Impairment Group, Fiscal Years 2000 to 2011

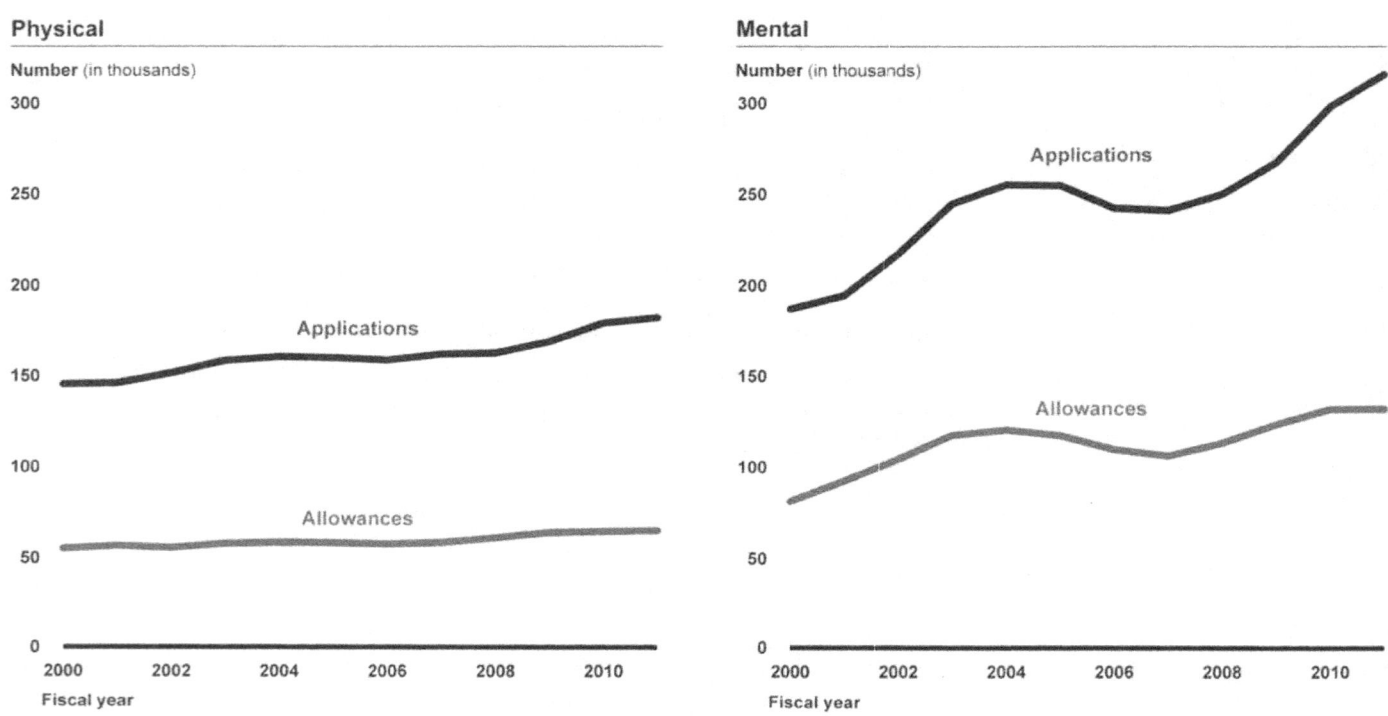

Source: GAO analysis of SSA data from the 831 Disability file.

Note: The information highlighted in this graphic is based on the primary impairment code recorded in the disability determination. Data represented as "applications" reflect SSI benefit claims where an initial disability determination decision was made each year. Some applications could have more than one determination if selected for a quality review or if the disability claim is updated during the same year. Such determinations are reflected in the data presented in the figure.

SSA data show that, for those children with mental impairments who apply, the number of children found medically eligible for benefits has increased for almost every mental impairment category—such as speech and language delay and mood disorder—for fiscal years 2000 to 2010, with the exception of intellectual disability.[29] SSA data also show that the three most prevalent primary mental impairments among those children found medically eligible in fiscal year 2011 were for (1) ADHD, (2) speech

---

[29]In accordance with Rosa's Law, "intellectual disability" has generally replaced the term "mental retardation." Pub. L. No. 111-256, 124 Stat. 2643.

GAO-12-497 Supplemental Security Income

and language delay, and (3) autism.[30] Of these impairments, SSA data indicate that applications and allowances for autism saw the largest percentage increases from fiscal years 2000 to 2011 (see fig. 3). (See app. III for trend information related to these three impairments.)

Figure 3: Initial Level Allowances for SSI Children with Mental Impairments, by Primary Impairment, Fiscal Years 2000 to 2011

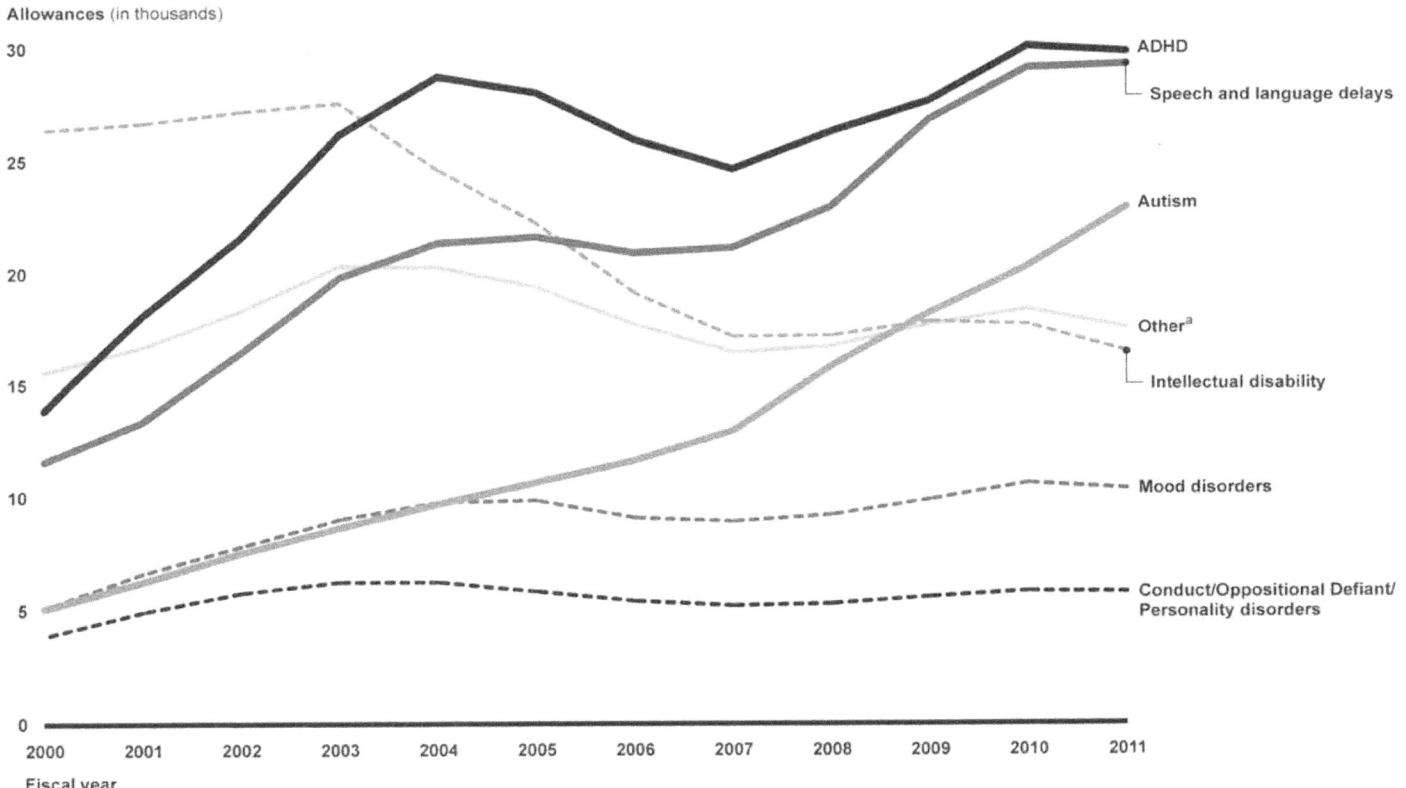

Source: GAO analysis of SSA data from the 831 Disability file.

Note: The information highlighted in this graphic is based on the primary impairment code recorded in the disability determination.

[30]These data are based on the primary impairment as designated by the DDS examiner. The recorded primary impairment code identifies the primary impairment used in the medical determination for an individual's eligibility for SSI disability benefits. These data appear in SSA's 831 and 832/833 Disability files. However, SSA officials have acknowledged that the primary codes are sometimes missing or inaccurately coded, with an estimated error rate of 5 to 6 percent.

SSA data also show that the cumulative numbers of children receiving SSI benefit payments due to a mental impairment has steadily increased. From December 2000 to December 2011, the total number of children with mental impairments on the SSI disability rolls grew almost 60 percent, from about 543,000 to almost 861,000 (see fig. 4).[31] Even though the cumulative number of children on the rolls has reached an all-time high, SSA data indicate that the percentage of children awarded SSI benefits each year due to a mental impairment has remained relatively stable, averaging about 65 percent from 2000 to 2011.

[31]The number of adults receiving SSI benefits has also steadily increased over the past decade. As of December 2011, 6.8 million adults were receiving SSI disability benefits, up from 5.8 million as of December 2000.

Figure 4: Number of Children under Age 18 Receiving Federally Administered SSI Payments, by Mental and Physical Impairment Group, December 2000 through December 2011

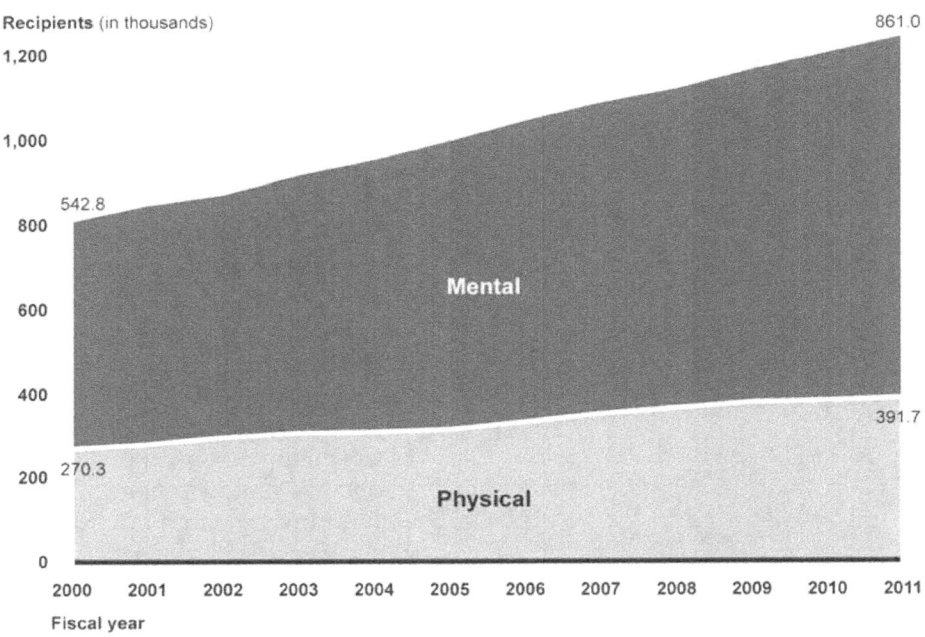

Source: GAO analysis of SSA data from the Supplemental Security Record.

Note: This figure does not include those diagnostic groups that SSA reported as "unknown." SSA data showed that as of December 2000, "unknowns" totaled 33,042 children (4 percent of all children), and as of December 2011, 24,443 children (2 percent of all children).

Additional information on trends in the numbers of SSI applications, allowances, and benefit receipts for children with mental impairments for individual U.S. states can be found in an electronic supplement to this report.[32]

---

[32]See GAO, *Supplemental Security Income: State Trends in Applications, Allowances, and Benefit Receipts for Children with Mental Impairments, an E-Supplement to GAO-12-497*, GAO-12-498SP (Washington, D.C.: June 26, 2012).

GAO-12-497 Supplemental Security Income

Several Factors May Contribute to the Growth in Numbers of Children Applying for and Receiving SSI Benefits

We previously reported that various factors—such as expanded disability standards and major program outreach—contributed to rapid growth in the SSI children caseload during the 1990s.[33] At that time, we also reported that various factors contributed to growth in the total number of SSI recipients, such as fraud and abuse, immigration, and the economy. Some research suggests additional factors may be currently affecting the growth and composition of childhood disability applicants and recipients, especially for those children with mental impairments. Some of these factors may include, but are not limited to:

- *Increased number of children living in poverty in United States.* The number of children who are financially eligible for SSI benefits may have increased because the number of children living in poverty has increased significantly over the past decade. From 2000 to 2010, the overall poverty rate for children increased from 16 (11.6 million) to 22 percent (16.4 million).[34] In addition, research has shown that certain impairments are more prevalent among children in low-income households. For example, the prevalence of ADHD among children during the period between 2007 and 2009 was 7.9 percent for children with a family income of 200 percent or more of the poverty level, whereas the incidence of ADHD was 10.3 percent for children with a family income of less than 100 percent of the poverty level, according to the National Center on Health Statistics.[35]

- *Increased awareness and improved diagnosis of certain mental impairments.* The increased awareness and improved diagnosis of

---

[33]GAO, *Supplemental Security Income: Growth and Changes in Recipient Population Call for Reexamining Program,* GAO/HEHS-95-137 (Washington, D.C.: July 1995); *Social Security: Federal Disability Programs Face Major Issues,* GAO/T-HEHS-95-97 (Washington, D.C.: Mar. 2, 1995); and *Social Security: Rapid Rise in Children on SSI Disability Rolls Follows New Regulations,* GAO/HEHS-94-225 (Washington, D.C.: September 1994).

[34]U.S. Department of Commerce, Economics and Statistics Administration, U.S. Census Bureau, *Income, Poverty, and Health Insurance Coverage in the United States: 2010* (September 2011), and *Poverty in the United States: 2000* (September 2001).

[35]U.S. Department of Health and Human Services, Centers for Disease Control and Prevention, National Center for Health Statistics, *Attention Deficit Hyperactivity Disorder Among Children Age 5-17 in the United States, 1998-2009,* NCHS Data Brief, No. 70, (August 2011), and *Summary of Health Statistics for U.S. Children: National Health Interview Survey, 2010,* Vital and Health Statistics, Series 10, Number 250 (December 2011).

certain mental impairments in recent years may also be contributing to the growth among individual mental impairments, such as ADHD and autism. According to the Centers for Disease Controls and Prevention, about one in six U.S. children had a reported developmental disability from 2006 to 2008, which represents an increase of 17 percent from 1997 to 2008.[36] Researchers noted that the number of children with select developmental disabilities, such as ADHD and autism, has increased. They added that more study was needed to better understand the influence of factors, such as early intervention services, on the prevalence of developmental disabilities in recent years. Some disability advocates have also suggested that the increased prevalence of certain mental impairments may be due, in part, to a diagnostic shift in the general population, away from the less specific diagnosis of intellectual disability and toward more targeted diagnoses, such as autism and speech and language delay.

- *Increased numbers of previously uninsured children obtaining health care coverage.* Today, more low-income children may have access to health care coverage than in years past, potentially providing them with greater access to physicians and medical treatments and increased opportunities for diagnosis of a mental impairment. Since fiscal year 2000, Medicaid and the Children's Health Insurance Program (CHIP)—the nation's largest health care financing programs that can be accessed by low-income children—have insured an increasing number of children. In fact, from fiscal year 2000 to 2009, the number of children enrolled in Medicaid increased from about 24 million to 34 million, while during the same period, the number of children enrolled in CHIP increased from about 3.4 million to 7.7 million. According to the Kaiser Commission on Medicaid and the Uninsured, about 90 percent of all children in the United States had some type of health care coverage, with Medicaid and other public programs insuring about 35 percent of these children.[37]

- *Focus on identifying children with disabilities through public school special education services.* The Individuals with Disabilities Education

---

[36]Coleen A. Boyle, Sheree Boulet, Laura A. Schieve, Robin A. Cohen, Stephen J. Blumberg, Marshalyn Yeargin-Allsopp, Susanna Visser, and Michael D. Kogan. "Trends in the Prevalence of Developmental Disabilities in U.S. Children, 1997-2008," *Pediatrics*, vol. 127, no. 6 (May 23, 2011).

[37]Health Coverage of Children: The Role of Medicaid and CHIP, Kaiser Commission on Medicaid and the Uninsured, February 2011.

Act (IDEA), as reauthorized in 2004, allows school districts to use some of their IDEA funding for early intervening services for students who have not been identified as needing special education, but who need additional academic and behavioral support.[38] Some special education practitioners we interviewed believe that this expansion of services to children not previously identified as having a disability might cause parents to mistakenly conclude that their children have a disability and are therefore eligible for SSI benefits. While many children may be receiving services under IDEA,[39] children would not necessarily qualify for SSI benefits given that "disability" is defined differently under the Social Security Act and IDEA and they may not meet the financial eligibility criteria for SSI.

- *Fewer children leaving the disability program prior to age 18.* In recent years, SSA has conducted significantly fewer childhood CDRs. As a result, the number of children who remain on the SSI benefit rolls each year has increased because fewer children are being removed from the disability program prior to age 18.

While each of these factors may contribute to the overall program growth, the relative effects of these and other factors are not fully known, and were beyond the scope of this report. Also, the overall child population in the United States has grown since 2000 and the demographics of this population may have changed since that time.

---

[38]Pub. L. No. 108-446, 118 Stat. 2647 and 20 U.S.C. § 1413(f). IDEA authorizes federal funding to states for special education and related services, and for the states that accept these funds, sets out principles under which special education and related services are to be provided. See 20 U.S.C. § 1400 et seq. IDEA requires that each child with a disability have an individualized education program, and children with disabilities may also receive related services, including speech-language pathology and audiology services, physical therapy, and nursing.

[39]According to the U.S. Department of Education, more than 6 million children aged 6 to 21 received special education services under IDEA, Part B, in the fall of 2006. U.S. Department of Education, Office of Special Education and Rehabilitative Services, *30th Annual Report to Congress on the Implementation of the Individuals with Disabilities Education Act, 2008* (Washington, D.C.: December 2011).

GAO-12-497 Supplemental Security Income

Secondary Impairments Were Present for Many of Those Found Medically Eligible

For many children found medically eligible for SSI benefits, examiners cited a secondary impairment as evidence when making a determination. When evaluating how a child functions, examiners assess the interactive and cumulative effects of all of the impairments for which they have evidence, including those that are not considered severe,[40] and subsequently code those primary and secondary impairments relevant to the determination in their management system, whether the determination is allowed or denied. When we asked SSA to provide us with data on secondary impairments, officials said that there were significant inconsistencies in how examiners nationwide code these impairments, and said that we would need to review individual cases in order to reliably obtain information on secondary impairments.

To better understand what role secondary impairments play in the eligibility process, as well as the extent to which examiners used a combination of impairments to support determinations, we conducted a case file review of initial determinations when the primary impairment was ADHD, speech and language delay, or autism. We estimate that of the applicants found medically eligible in fiscal year 2010, 55 percent had a secondary impairment present, and of these cases, 94 percent of the secondary impairments were mental.[41] More specifically, of the ADHD cases DDS examiners allowed, 74 percent had a secondary impairment present, while 49 and 39 percent of autism and speech and language cases, respectively, had a secondary impairment present.[42]

We also found that when secondary impairments were present, examiners used functional equivalence as the basis for an allowance more often than they used meeting or medically equal the listings as the basis. Our case file review showed that examiners used a secondary impairment to support 49 percent of cases allowed on the basis of

---

[40]20 C.F.R. § 416.926a(a).

[41]Estimates based on our case file review are generalizeable only to initial determinations made in fiscal year 2010 for the three primary mental impairments most frequently allowed for benefits—ADHD, speech and language delay, and autism. Unless otherwise noted, the 95 percent margins of error for these estimates are plus or minus 8 percentage points.

[42]The 95 percent margins of error for percentages in this paragraph range from plus or minus 10 to plus or minus 14 percentage points.

functional equivalence, but only 22 percent of cases allowed on the basis of meeting or medically equaling the listings.[43]

The presence of multiple impairments may explain why examiners have allowed an increasing number of ADHD, speech and language delay, and autism cases using functional equivalence as a basis for the determination. Determining disability for children with impairments that are not severe enough to match a listed impairment can be subjective. In order to make a disability determination on the basis of functional equivalence, examiners must gather extensive evidence from both medical and nonmedical sources, including teachers, parents, and others knowledgeable about the child's day-to-day behavior and activities. The examiner is then required to classify the child's limitation into certain areas or domains of functioning, such as acquiring and using information and interacting with others. This process requires DDS examiners to make a series of judgments, because these domains of functioning may be closely interrelated and impairments may or may not affect functioning in more than one area. Nevertheless, examiners' use of functional equivalence as a basis for determinations has steadily increased for more than a decade for those impairments we reviewed. In fiscal year 2011, 71 percent of recipient children with ADHD were allowed on this basis, compared to 23 percent in fiscal year 2000. Eighty-one percent of children with speech and language delays were allowed on the basis of functional equivalence in fiscal year 2011, an increase from 59 percent in fiscal year 2000. Compared to ADHD and speech and language delay, the percentage of autism recipients allowed on the basis of functional equivalence is lower—30 percent in fiscal year 2011—but this still represented an increase from the 9 percent allowed on this basis in fiscal year 2000.

While it appears that DDS examiners consider secondary impairments when making a determination as evidenced by our case file review, SSA officials told us that DDS examiners do not always consistently and accurately code secondary impairment data, which they acknowledged prevents them from fully understanding trends in the disability determination process. We found in our case file review that examiners sometimes code a secondary impairment that was alleged by a claimant,

---

[43]The 95 percent margins of error for percentages for these data range from plus or minus 5 to plus or minus 11 percentage points.

GAO-12-497 Supplemental Security Income

but not material to the ultimate determination. For example, examiners coded a secondary impairment that they did not use as support in 27 of 80 allowance cases for which a secondary impairment was present. SSA officials told us that with better information on secondary impairments they could compare trends for decisions with single and multiple impairments, and better target CDRs towards those impairments most likely to improve over time. Officials attributed the coding errors primarily to a lack of understanding among examiners about the importance of impairment coding, and said that the agency was taking steps, such as issuing revised guidance and developing trainings, to clarify the importance of capturing such information. However, officials said that improving proper coding holds a lower priority among its competing workloads.

Examiners Rely on a Combination of Key Information Sources to Determine Medical Eligibility

DDS examiners rely on a combination of key medical and nonmedical information sources—such as medical records, effects of prescribed medications, school records, and teacher and parent assessments—in determining a child's medical eligibility for benefits.[44] Several DDS officials we interviewed said that when making a determination, they consider the totality of information related to the child's impairments, rather than one piece of information in isolation.[45] Based on our case file review, we estimate that examiners generally cited four to five information sources as support for their decisions in fiscal year 2010 for the three most prevalent mental impairments.[46] While examiners relied on multiple information sources, we found that the extent they used these sources varied (see fig. 5).

---

[44] For more information, see 20 C.F.R. § 416.913.

[45] For more information, see 20 C.F.R. § 416.924(a).

[46] Specifically, the mean number of sources was 4.6 (plus or minus 0.2).

Figure 5: Information Sources Used to Support Determinations for Children with Alleged ADHD, Speech and Language Delay, and Autism, Fiscal Year 2010

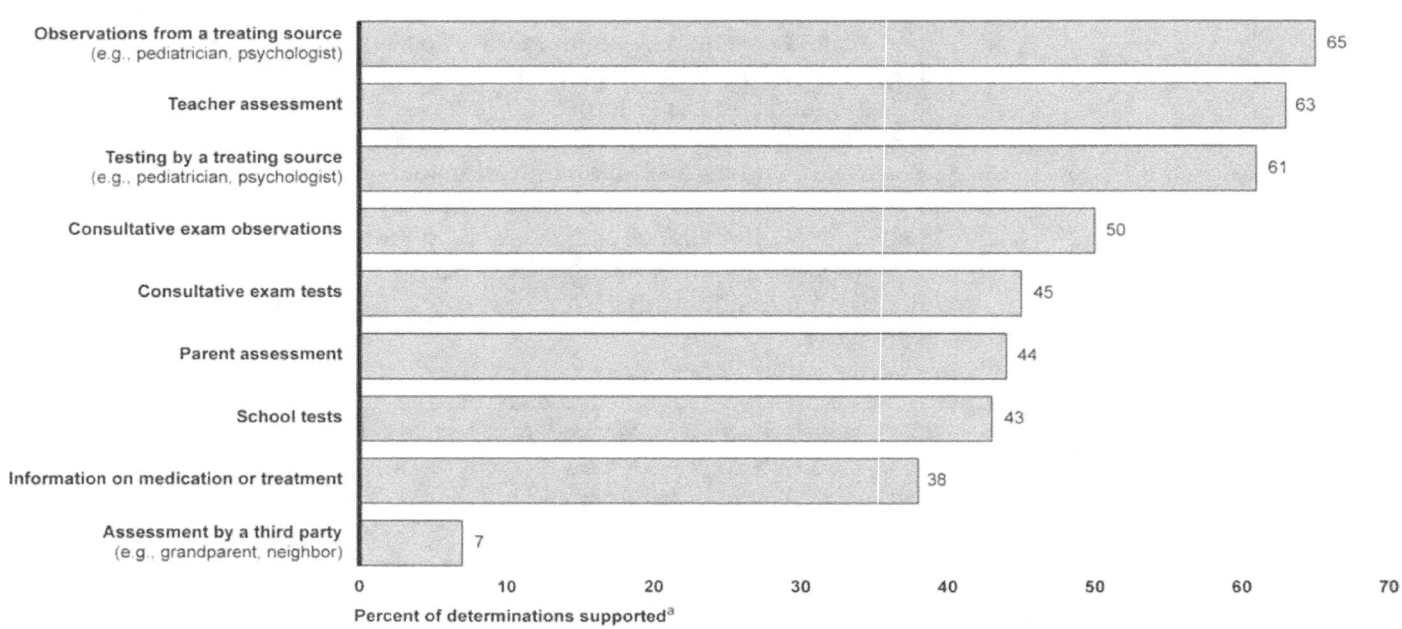

Percent of determinations supported[a]

Source: GAO estimates based on case file review of sampled initial determinations for children with alleged ADHD, speech and language delay, and autism, fiscal year 2010.

[a]The 95 percent margin of error for these estimates does not exceed plus or minus 7 percentage points.

In more than 90 percent of the cases we reviewed, the examiner used some form of medical evidence to support the decision, regardless of whether the child's impairment met, medically equaled, or functionally equaled the listings. SSA generally requires DDS examiners to assist children and their parents or guardians in obtaining medical records in an effort to develop at least a 1-year-long medical history prior to applying for benefits.[47] We estimate that examiners used observations from a treating source, such as a pediatrician or psychologist, about a child's functioning and testing by a treating source as support for 65 percent and 61 percent of their determinations, respectively, making them among the most commonly cited information sources. According to many of the DDS officials we interviewed, examiners attempt to obtain medical evidence,

---

[47]20 C.F.R. § 416.912(d).

such as psychological tests, physician's notes, and mental health records, for children with alleged mental impairments.

If such evidence is not available or is inconclusive, DDS examiners may purchase a consultative exam to provide additional medical evidence and help them establish the severity of a child's impairment.[48] This examination is intended to provide the additional medical evidence, such as results of a physical examination and laboratory findings, needed for a determination. Based on our case file review, we estimate at least one consultative examination was present in 52 percent of the cases. In some cases, DDS offices requested multiple consultative examinations, such as both a psychological and speech and language evaluation to address different aspects of the alleged impairment. Consultative examinations also provide information on the severity of the child's impairment. For example, one examination provider described a case in which a child with a speech and language delay had receptive and expressive language skills that were nearly 2 years behind his chronological age. We estimated that cases were more likely to be allowed if the consultative exam provider described the child's impairment as severe. However, many DDS officials told us that such examinations are only a "snap-shot" in time and do not provide a longitudinal view of the child's functioning. For this reason, some DDS officials said that information from a treating source with a long-standing relationship with the child, such as a physician, is more useful.

In addition to medical evidence, SSA uses nonmedical information to evaluate the severity of the child's impairment and functioning as part of the eligibility determination.[49] These sources include parents, day care providers, teachers, and others knowledgeable about the child's day-to-day behavior and activities. SSA field office staff may also provide observations about the child, if the child is present for the disability interview. (We estimate about 8 percent of child applicants were present at the field office for the disability interview.)

---

[48] 20 C.F.R. § 416.917.

[49] 20 C.F.R. § 416.924a.

Several DDS officials told us school records and teacher assessments (standardized questionnaires)[50] are especially critical for determining medical eligibility because these assessments provide information on a child's functioning over time and are generally more objective than parent assessments. According to some DDS examiners, parents primarily observe their child in an unstructured home environment after the child's medications have worn off, and may not know what behaviors are developmentally normal, whereas teachers are generally in a position to compare the child to other children and provide neutral observations on how the child relates to peers, responds to medication, and performs in school. We estimate teacher assessments and school testing were used to support 63 and 43 percent of determinations, respectively. We also identified several examples in the case files we reviewed where the teacher's assessment was used to establish the child's level of functioning and response to medication. For example:

- To support an allowance in one autism case, the examiner noted "Per teacher, he is virtually nonverbal. The teacher confirms he is not toilet trained or independent in any area of self care."

- To support a denial decision in one ADHD case, the examiner noted that the teacher's assessment indicated that the child's medication "has 'helped tremendously' with [the child's] ability to concentrate." Additionally, according to the teacher the child "has many friends and is very social. She has no problems interacting with others. Claimant has no problems with self care. She participates in the softball and dance team."

- To support a denial decision in one autism case, the examiner reported that the "teacher...notes he is more controlled on his meds."

After the necessary information is collected to make a disability determination, several examiners said that they compare all the information to identify inconsistencies and assign weight to the various sources. For example, some officials told us examiners assess the credibility of parents' assessments of children's functioning by comparing it to physicians' and teachers' statements. SSA policy notes that an

---

[50]The standardized SSA teacher questionnaire includes checkboxes and multiple choice questions and is organized into sections that cover broad domains of functioning, such as acquiring and using information and attending and completing tasks.

inconsistency does not necessarily mean that a determination cannot be made because often most of the evidence or the most substantial evidence outweighs the inconsistent evidence and additional information would not change the determination or decision. Among the 298 alleged ADHD, speech and language delay, and autism cases we examined, there were 25 in which material inconsistencies could not be resolved between sources, requiring the examiner to assign more or less weight to certain sources. Examiners assigned more weight to teacher assessments or information from school testing in 11 of the 25 cases. Examiners also generally assigned more weight to testing and observations of functioning by a consultative examiner (10 of the 25 cases) or by a treating source (10 of the 25 cases). In contrast, parents' assessments were given less weight in 14 of the 25 cases, although decisions were made on a case by case basis. In one ADHD case, the child's mother alleged a developmental delay, but a psychological consultative exam did not find evidence of such a delay. The child's teacher also stated that the child performed well academically when not under timed conditions. In this case, the examiner gave less weight to the parent's assessment and denied the claim.

When Used in Eligibility Decisions, Medication and Treatment Information Is Frequently a Basis for Denying Benefits

Despite a media report that prescription medication is considered by some parents as key to obtaining SSI benefits, we found that medication and treatment information is frequently a basis for denying benefits. SSA and DDS officials told us that medication is generally given no more weight than any other medical or nonmedical information in determining a child's medical eligibility. In addition, several DDS officials told us medication is considered in the context of other sources of information as "just one piece of the puzzle." Our case file review confirmed that information on medication and treatment was never the sole source of support for an allowance or denial. In fact, we found that applicants were more likely to be denied than allowed when medication was reported (see fig. 6).

Figure 6: Allowances and Denials by Medication Status for Children with Alleged ADHD, Speech and Language Delay, and Autism, Fiscal Year 2010

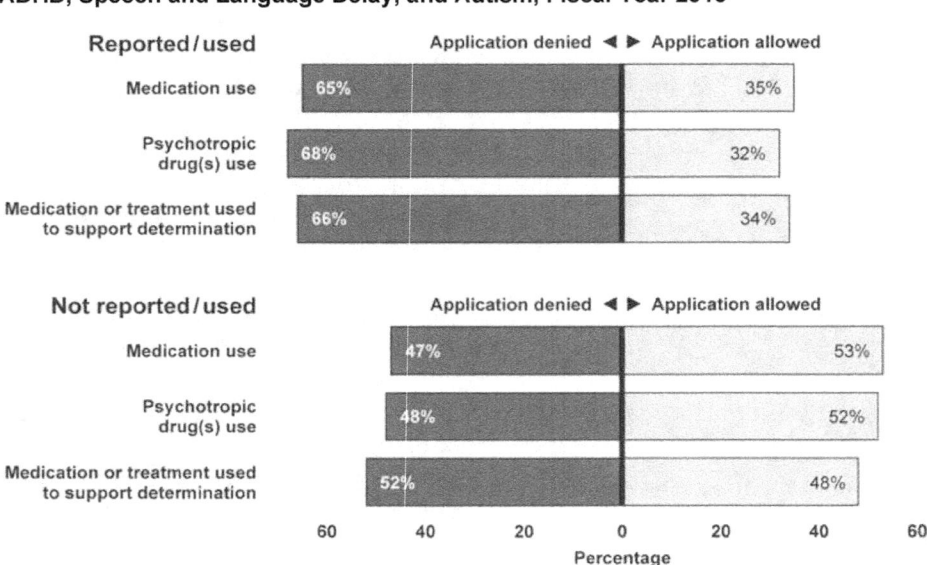

Source: GAO estimates based on case file review of sampled fiscal year 2010 initial determinations for children with alleged ADHD, speech and languge delay, and autism.

When applying for benefits, parents reported that their children were prescribed some form of medication in 58 percent of the cases we reviewed. Of cases where medication was reported as present, 65 percent were denied and 35 percent were allowed. By comparison, 47 percent of cases were denied and 53 percent were allowed when medication was not reported as present.[51] We found that in cases in which psychotropic drug use was reported,[52] applicants were also more likely to be denied.[53] In these cases, 68 percent were denied and 32 percent were allowed. Nevertheless, our case file review suggests

---

[51]The difference in the proportion allowed between cases with and without medication was statistically distinguishable at the 0.05 level. The 95 percent margins of error for percentages in this paragraph range from plus or minus 5 to plus or minus 8 percentage points.

[52]Psychotropic drugs, such as antidepressants and antipsychotics, affect brain activity associated with mental processes and behavior.

[53]For more detailed information on applicants' reported medication and psychotropic drug use, see appendix IV.

GAO-12-497 Supplemental Security Income

examiners did not decide whether to allow or deny a claim based on the absence or presence of medication. Although medication was reported as present in 58 percent of cases, it was only cited as support for a determination in 38 percent of cases.

Beyond examining cases where parents reported that their children were prescribed medication, we also specifically looked at cases where examiners cited information on medication or treatment as part of the rationale for their determinations. We found examiners generally considered how the child responded to these interventions when making a determination, and in 66 percent of the cases where information on medication or treatment was used to support a determination, the applicant was denied. When examiners cited medication and treatment as a basis for denials, they noted that the child's functioning improved due to these interventions. For example, in one denied ADHD case, the examiner wrote that the claimant "has responded well to medication and while on medication has no problems functioning, completing work on time and getting along with others." In one denied speech and language delay case, the examiner noted that the claimant "has been through multiple therapies" and that "[t]hese therapies have been successful." To the extent that medication improves functioning, DDS officials told us they could potentially find that the child is not disabled under program rules. In contrast, in cases where the child's functioning was not improved by medication, this information generally helped support an allowance. For example, in one allowed ADHD case, the examiner noted that the child was "[n]ot able to complete work independently despite tx [treatment] with psych meds and special supervision in a partial [classroom] inclusion setting." In another allowed ADHD case, the examiner observed that both the treating source and teacher's assessment "indicate marked limitations in attention and concentration even with stimulant meds."

Despite the examiners' focus on how medication affects functioning, certain field office and DDS officials acknowledged that they believe some parents are under the impression that medicating their children will improve their likelihood of being found eligible for benefits. For example, in one denied ADHD case the child's mother did not cooperate with the DDS's efforts to obtain a consultative exam.[54] The mother argued the

---

[54]This case was not part of our case file review, but SSA provided us with information on it.

DDS should already have enough evidence to support an allowance because the child was taking medication. However, other DDS officials told us some parents may avoid medicating their child prior to a consultative examination so that the child misbehaves and appears more disabled—further reinforcing the importance of multiple tests and observations for determining eligibility.

Examiners Sometimes Lack Complete Information to Inform Their Decision Making and Identify Potential Threats to Program Integrity

Despite the importance of nonmedical information in determining a child's medical eligibility, examiners sometimes face challenges obtaining complete information. Several DDS offices reported difficulty obtaining school records or teacher assessments, which they partly attributed to school and teacher concerns about the time involved to compile this information, potential liability issues, or confusion about how such information is used in the disability decision-making process. For example, some DDS examiners told us that in certain instances teachers view their completion of the assessment as affirming that a child is disabled and thus endorsing SSA's decision to award benefits. They do not understand that examiners base their determinations on the totality of evidence or that the assessment could be used to support a denial. In one of the cases we reviewed, a teacher returned a blank teacher assessment with a note stating "we are not allowed to fill these out anymore."

Our case file review estimated that teacher assessments were absent for 57 percent of cases for children age 7 or younger—which is unsurprising, given that many of these children may not yet be school age—but such assessments were also absent for 25 percent of cases for children older than age 7. To address this challenge, SSA officials told us that some DDS offices have dedicated staff to conduct outreach to schools in order to emphasize the importance of information from schools as an evidence source. However, they added that these staff have competing priorities, including recruiting consultative exam providers and other medical professionals, which limit the amount of outreach they can perform. In addition to strengthening relationships with school personnel, disability advocates told us that SSA could revise the teacher assessment by using clearer language to make it more inviting to teachers. They also noted that SSA could further emphasize that by completing the assessment, teachers are not endorsing SSA's ultimate decision as to whether the child is disabled or qualifies for benefits. Because schools and teachers are not required to provide records or teacher assessments, some DDS offices pay a fee for school records, but state laws prevent others from doing so, according to SSA officials. SSA officials did not know the extent to which DDS offices have paid for school records or the amount they had paid. [55]

SSA officials informed us they have heard reports of some DDS offices facing challenges in obtaining information from schools, but they do not know the degree to which these challenges exist nationwide, nor has SSA conducted an empirical analysis of challenges related to obtaining information from schools. SSA did issue guidance on steps DDS offices can take to mitigate processing delays associated with obtaining school evidence during extended school breaks, such as summer vacation, but the agency has not issued guidance regarding year-round challenges associated with obtaining information from schools. Without further study to determine how widespread these obstacles are, it will remain unclear whether additional guidance is warranted.

In addition to the challenges they sometimes face in obtaining information from schools, DDS examiners said that they do not routinely receive information from SSA field offices on multiple siblings receiving SSI benefits within the same household even though they are directed to be alert for such cases. SSA's policy operations manual states that disabilities may occur in more than one member of a family or household, but notes prior case experience has shown this type of situation is an indicator of possible fraud or abuse, particularly where certain mental impairments are involved. For example, one of SSA's Cooperative Disability Investigations Units investigated a case in which parents applied for SSI benefits on behalf of their four children, alleging that they all suffered from ADHD and conduct issues. [56] However, investigators found that the school guidance counselor had never observed them exhibiting symptoms of ADHD despite seeing the four children daily, and that a doctor had rescinded an order authorizing the school to administer ADHD medication to the children. In this instance, SSA subsequently denied the siblings' applications for SSI benefits. SSA's policy operations manual directs examiners to refer such cases to SSA's Cooperative Disability Investigations Unit or Office of the Inspector General for further

---

[55]The 95 percent margin of error for percentages in this paragraph range from plus or minus 9 to plus or minus 10 percentage points.

[56]The Cooperative Disability Investigations Program, which is managed by SSA's Office of Operations and Office of Inspector General, is responsible for investigating questions of fraud in SSA's disability programs.

development, if questionable issues cannot be resolved. Based on our interviews, it appears that SSA field offices do not consistently notify DDS examiners when an applicant's siblings are already receiving SSI benefits, nor are they always made aware of concurrent sibling applications. SSA data indicate that as of January 2012, nearly 64,000 children, or 5 percent of all child recipients, resided in a household where more than 1 child received disability benefits. Without information on such children, DDS examiners may be limited in their ability to identify potential fraud or abuse in the program and elevate these cases to the attention of SSA's fraud investigations unit.

SSA Has Conducted Few Childhood CDRs in Recent Years

SSA has conducted significantly fewer CDRs for children receiving SSI benefits since 2000, even though SSA is generally required to perform CDRs at least every 3 years on child recipients under age 18 whose impairments are likely to improve, as well as certain other individuals (see fig 7).[57] Childhood CDRs overall fell from more than 150,000 in fiscal year 2000 to about 45,000 reviews in fiscal year 2011 (a 70 percent decrease). More specifically, CDRs for children under age 18 with mental impairments declined from more than 84,000 to about 16,000 (an 80 percent decrease). Similarly, SSA has conducted significantly fewer CDRs for adult benefit recipients of either SSI or Social Security Disability Insurance (SSDI).[58] From fiscal years 2000 to 2011, the number of adult

---

[57]Under Title XVI of the Social Security Act, SSA is generally required to (1) conduct a CDR at least every 3 years on all child recipients under age 18 whose impairments are likely to improve (or, at the Commissioner's option, recipients whose impairments are unlikely to improve) (42 U.S.C. § 1382c(a)(3)(H)(ii)(I)); (2) conduct a CDR within 12 months after the birth of a child who was granted benefits in part because of low birth weight (42 U.S.C. § 1382c(a)(3)(H)(iv)); and (3) redetermine, within 1 year of the individual's 18th birthday (or whenever the Commissioner determines the individual is subject to a redetermination), the eligibility of any individual who was eligible for SSI childhood payments in the month before attaining age 18, by applying the criteria used in determining initial eligibility for adults (42 U.S.C. § 1382c(a)(3)(H)(iii)). For children under the age of 18—except for the initial CDR for low birth weight babies—DDS offices are directed by SSA policy to determine when recipients will be due for CDRs on the basis of their potential for medical improvement, and select and schedule a review date—otherwise known as a "diary date"—for each recipient's CDR.

[58]The SSDI program provides benefits to eligible individuals who meet certain minimum work requirements.

CDRs fell from 584,000 to 179,000.[59] However, in comparison, the proportion of childhood CDRs conducted has remained much lower than the proportion of adult CDRs conducted. SSA officials attribute the decrease in CDRs overall, including childhood CDRs for those with mental impairments, primarily to resource limitations and a greater emphasis on processing initial claims and reducing the backlog of requests for appeals hearings in recent years. While SSA did increase the number of CDRs it performed after receiving additional funding specifically targeted for CDRs from fiscal years 1996 to 2002, CDRs decreased once the funding expired.

[59]For adults receiving SSI, SSA conducts CDRs using two methods: (1) SSA headquarters sends some cases to the DDS for a full medical review, and (2) SSA mails a questionnaire to other recipients and reviews their responses to determine continued eligibility. At this time, SSA does not use the mailer process for SSI child recipients. For comparability in the number of CDRs for adults and children, the CDR data in this section apply to full medical reviews only.

Figure 7: Number of Childhood CDRs Conducted for SSI Recipients under Age 18, by Primary Impairment, Fiscal Years 2000 through 2011

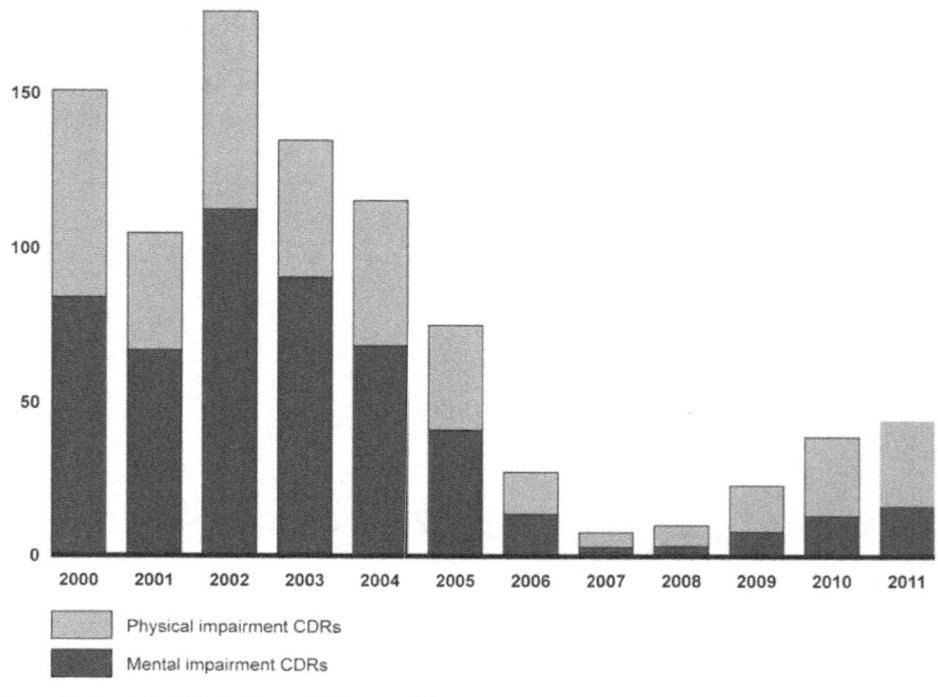

CDRs (in thousands)

Physical impairment CDRs

Mental impairment CDRs

Source: GAO analysis of SSA data from the CDR Waterfall Files.

Hundreds of Thousands of Childhood CDRs Are Overdue by More than 3 Years, Including Reviews for Children Expected to Medically Improve

Because SSA has conducted fewer childhood CDRs in recent years, as of August 1, 2011,[60] the agency had a backlog of about 435,000 child SSI recipients with mental impairments whose review had not yet been conducted (see fig. 8).[61] Of these recipients, about 344,000 (79 percent) had exceeded the scheduled date by at least a year, with about 205,000 (47 percent) exceeding their date by 3 years and about 24,000 (6 percent) exceeding the scheduled date by 6 years. We also identified several cases which exceeded their scheduled date by 13 years or more. SSA data also indicate that while age 18 redeterminations are conducted in a more timely manner, about 8 percent of these reviews are also overdue by 3 years or more for recipients with mental impairments.[62]

---

[60]SSA conducts an annual analysis of pending CDRs for children. This is the most recent date for which these data are available.

[61]A total of about 861,000 child recipients with mental impairments were receiving SSI benefits as of December 2011.

[62]SSA informed us that 95.6 percent of the age 18 redeterminations are released to the field offices for processing by SSA headquarters within two months of the recipients' 18th birthday, and most all of them were released by no later than their 19th birthday.

GAO-12-497 Supplemental Security Income

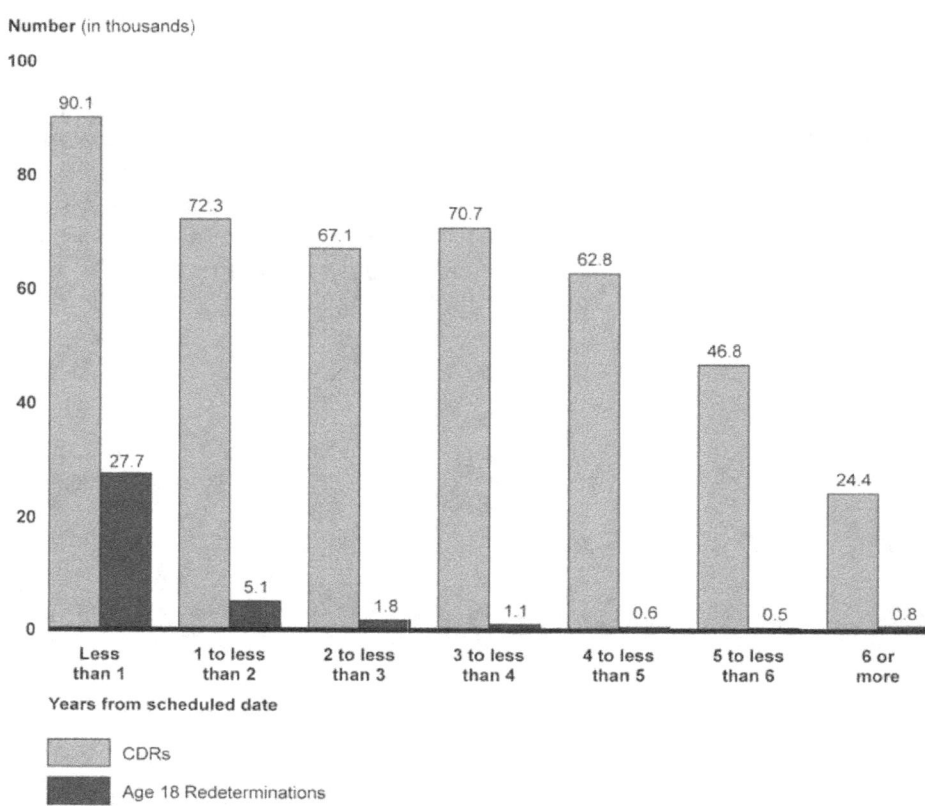

Figure 8: Pending Childhood CDRs and Age 18 Redeterminations for Those with Mental Impairments, by Time Lapsed, as of August 1, 2011

Number (in thousands)

CDRs

Age 18 Redeterminations

Source: GAO analysis of SSA data from the CDR Waterfall Files.

Upon further review of the 24,000 childhood CDRs pending 6 years or more, we found that about 70 percent were for children deemed "medical improvement possible," while 25 percent of these pending CDRs were for those children deemed medically expected to improve (see fig. 9). As we noted, DDS staff generally establish the timeframe for when SSA should conduct a CDR on the basis of the expected likelihood of a recipient's medical improvement. The improvement categories and general time frames used are (1) "medical improvement expected," 6 to 18 months; (2) "medical improvement possible," 3 years; and (3) "medical improvement not expected," 5 to 7 years. Among childhood CDRs, reviews of children who are expected to medically improve are more productive than reviews of children who are not expected to medically improve because they have a greater likelihood of benefit cessation and thus yield higher cost savings over time. In total, almost all of the more than 24,000 CDRs pending for 6 years or more fell within the improvement categories of "medical improvement expected" or "medical improvement possible," and, surprisingly, about 6,200 of these were pending for children who had been expected to medically improve. In fact, we identified nine recipients who were expected to medically improve, but whose CDR had been pending for 13 years or more.

Figure 9: Childhood CDRs Pending for at Least 6 Years, by Anticipated Medical Improvement Category, for Children with Mental Impairments, as of August 1, 2011

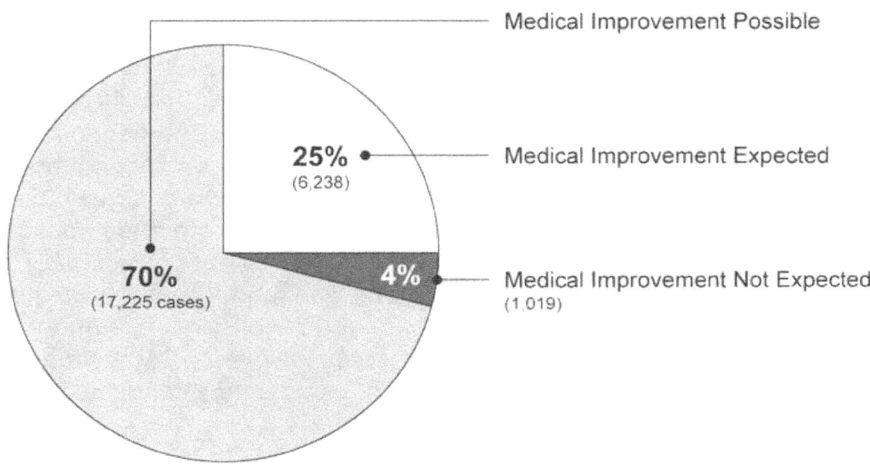

Source: GAO analysis of SSA data from the CDR Waterfall Files.

Note: Percentages do not equal 100 percent due to rounding.

Due to Competing Workloads, SSA Gives Lower Priority to Most Childhood CDRs, Including Legally Required Reviews for Children Likely to Medically Improve

According to SSA officials, when CDR funding is less than what is needed to conduct all CDRs at the scheduled intervals, the agency has historically given priority to (1) maintaining SSDI CDR currency, (2) performing statutorily mandated SSI age 18 and low birth weight reviews, and (3) performing reviews considered most cost-effective. As a result, SSA has not conducted many other types of the statutorily mandated SSI reviews and childhood CDRs in recent years. SSA officials also told us that it is more cost effective to conduct adult SSDI CDRs than childhood SSI CDRs, because ceasing benefits for a young adult recipient may potentially represent decades of saved benefits. Additionally, because SSDI benefit payments are, on average, almost twice as much as SSI childhood payments, CDRs of adult SSDI cases generally produce greater lifetime savings, according to SSA officials. However, SSA only ceased about 12 percent of all adult claims that received a CDR, compared to 32 percent of children, in fiscal year 2011. More specifically, of those childhood CDRs conducted for children under age 18 with mental impairments, SSA ceased benefits for about 28 percent on average in fiscal year 2011, with personality disorders[63] and speech and language delay having the highest cessation rates, 39 and 38 percent, respectively.[64]

SSA places a high priority on conducting certain SSI reviews, such as age 18 redeterminations and CDRs of low birth weight babies. SSA is generally required by law to conduct age 18 redeterminations within 1 year after a child turns age 18, and within 12 months after birth for recipients whose low birth weight was a contributing factor material to the determination of their disability.[65] In fiscal year 2011, CDRs in these two areas represented 82 percent of all childhood reviews. SSA officials told us that if resources are subsequently available after addressing these priority areas, they will conduct other SSI childhood CDRs. SSA uses a profiling model to score and prioritize the performance of CDRs for each recipient group by the probability of medical improvement for each recipient. The model contains 85 independent variables, including age, primary and secondary impairment, time on disability rolls, and medical diary type. However, SSA has maintained that due to limited CDR funding in recent years, it has conducted relatively few childhood CDRs based on this model.

The Social Security Act generally requires that SSA conduct CDRs, no less frequently than once every 3 years, for children under the age of 18

---

[63]Personality disorders are manifested by pervasive, inflexible, and maladaptive personality traits, which are typical of the child's long-term functioning and not limited to discrete episodes of illness. 20 C.F.R. pt. 404, subpt. P, app. 1.

[64]The 32 and 28 percent, respectively, of recipients reflect "initial cessations," meaning that the agency concluded at the end of the CDR that the claimant involved no longer met the eligibility standards to continue receiving benefits, and therefore started the process to cease benefits. Claimants may subsequently avail themselves of an appeals process, which can result in a reversal of the initial cessation.

[65]42 U.S.C. § 1382c(a)(3)(H)(iii) and (iv), respectively.

GAO-12-497 Supplemental Security Income

receiving SSI benefits who are likely to medically improve.[66] While SSA has the authority to waive this requirement on a state-by-state basis, SSA officials informed us that the agency has never formally exercised that authority. Consequently, SSA initially appeared to be in violation of the 3-year requirement set forth in the Social Security Act with respect to the more than 200,000 children we identified, as of August 1, 2011, for whom medical improvement was likely, but who had not received a CDR in the prior 3 years. Similarly, SSA's Office of the Inspector General recently reported that SSA had not complied with the childhood CDR provision in the Social Security Act.[67]

On February 23, 2012, we discussed with officials from SSA's Office of the General Counsel and the Office of Disability Programs whether the agency was in possible violation of the 3-year requirement, their views on the legal obligations to conduct CDRs, and whether the agency had ever exercised the waiver authority. SSA officials told us that they did not agree that the agency had failed to comply with this requirement. Rather, they explained that when SSA provides a DDS office funding that is not sufficient to cover its entire CDR caseload, that funding decision may functionally serve as a waiver of the 3-year requirement. However, they acknowledged that such funding decisions regarding state DDS offices would not in fact serve as a formal waiver under the law. We noted that, in fact, SSA's fiscal year 2009 CDR report indicated that the agency had not exercised its authority to waive the 3-year requirement.[68] In short, the answers provided to us during this discussion did not provide us with sufficient support for their position that the agency had exercised its waiver authority and, thereby, justified the practice of conducting significantly fewer CDRs than would otherwise be required by law.

---

[66] 42 U.S.C. § 1382c(a)(3)(H)(ii)(I). The relevant provision states the following: "Not less frequently than once every 3 years, the Commissioner shall review [...] the continued eligibility for benefits under this title of each individual who has not attained 18 years of age and is eligible for such benefits by reason of an impairment (or combination of impairments) which is likely to improve (or, at the option of the Commissioner, which is unlikely to improve)." According to its policy guidance, SSA defines both medical improvement expected and medical improvement possible cases as being cases likely to improve.

[67] Social Security Administration Office of the Inspector General, "Follow-Up: Childhood Continuing Disability Reviews and Age 18 Redeterminations" (A-01-11-11118), Sept. 23, 2011.

[68] This was the most recent annual CDR report available at the time of our discussion, in February 2012.

Therefore, we formally requested, in a letter dated March 6, 2012, that SSA's General Counsel provide us with the agency's official views on the issues of (1) their compliance with the CDR requirement, (2) their justification for not conducting certain childhood CDRs as required by law, and (3) whether the agency has exercised its waiver authority.

In response, SSA's General Counsel acknowledged, in a letter dated April 20, 2012, that there are at least 200,000 children in the SSI program under the age of 18 for whom medical improvement is likely, but who have not had a CDR in the last 3 years. They also noted that while the agency has not issued any documents that formally grant a "waiver" to a state, the agency believes the consultation process it engages in with each state is consistent with Congress' intent in enacting the waiver provision and is consistent with the agency's regulatory waiver provision.[69] Specifically, SSA informed us that the agency consults with the state DDS officials on a quarterly basis about how best to manage their workloads, including CDRs. In making determinations about the appropriate number of CDR cases to conduct, SSA noted that it considers the backlog of pending reviews, the projected number of new applications, the current and projected staffing levels in each state agency, and the available medical and other resources.[70] SSA maintains that these discussions are, in essence, an "informal" waiver process regarding the appropriate number of CDR cases that DDS officers should conduct.[71] In light of the questions we raised, SSA indicated it would begin issuing a formal waiver document after undertaking its ongoing

---

[69]20 C.F.R. § 416.990(g).

[70]The relevant provision of the law states that the 3-year requirement does not apply to the extent that the Commissioner of Social Security determines, on a state-by-state basis, that the requirement should be waived to ensure that only the appropriate number of such cases are reviewed, and states further that the Commissioner shall determine the appropriate number of cases to be reviewed based on many of these factors. 42 U.S.C. § 421(i)(2). The provision goes on to state that the Commissioner shall only provide for such a waiver if the state makes a good faith effort to meet proper staffing requirements for the state agency and to process case reviews in a timely fashion. The provision also requires the Commissioner to report annually to certain congressional committees about the waiver determinations SSA has made. Given the delays in SSA's response to our formal request for information, we were unable to solicit the information necessary to determine whether SSA is ensuring such good faith effort on the part of the states and whether SSA has been consistently reporting to Congress about its waiving of the 3 year requirement.

[71]SSA makes a distinction between a "formal" waiver that would be documented in writing and an "informal" waiver process based on its discussions with state officials regarding the appropriate number of CDR cases to review.

consultation process with the DDS offices, in order to make clear that it is complying with the requirements of the law. Specifically, SSA asserted that it would issue a written document to states that waives the requirement to perform all required CDRs when the appropriate number of cases that SSA expects the states to perform in a fiscal year is less than the total number of CDRs that will come due in the state during the relevant fiscal year.

In its most recent CDR report, which covers fiscal year 2010 and was dated May 1, 2012, SSA does not make a similar statement, as it did in the fiscal year 2009 report, that it had issued no waivers from the CDR requirements.[72] Rather, the agency explained its informal waiver process and the proposed issuance of a formal waiver document in the future, similar to its April 2012 letter, but with additional detail. The report indicated that the explanation is about the agency's "long-standing process;" however, SSA noted, that in previous annual CDR reports, the agency had not explained how it had met the waiver requirements. To make this point clearer, SSA proposed to begin issuing a formal waiver document in fiscal year 2012. We believe that there is some inconsistency about how SSA has described its waiver process, and thus its adherence to the law in the past, and the waiver process has not been transparent and open to date.

SSA's response noted that the agency intends to begin issuing a formal waiver document, but did not provide us with information on the extent to which the agency's waiver process would be open, transparent, and public. According to GAO's *Internal Control Management and Evaluation Tool*, agencies should maintain relevant and reliable information relating to their activities and should establish open and effective communications channels with relevant groups that could have an impact on agency activities, as well as establish communications with Congress, other federal agencies, the public, and others so that the agency's activities and risk are understood.[73] Without a transparent, open, and public waiver process, the extent to which SSA is conducting CDRs consistently with its legal requirements will continue to be unclear as it has been in the past.

---

[72]Social Security Administration, *Annual Report of Continuing Disability Reviews, Fiscal Year 2010* (May 1, 2012).

[73]GAO, *Internal Control Management and Evaluation Tool*, GAO-01-1008G (Washington, D.C.: August 2001).

In addition, it appears that SSA's Inspector General was not informed that the agency was exercising its waiver authority as it conducted its investigation, and as a result that office found SSA to be in violation of the 3-year requirement. Yet, SSA is now suggesting that its consultation process is, and has been, sufficient to satisfy the 3-year requirement. Until SSA formally clarifies how it will implement this waiver process, questions will remain about the extent to which the proposed waiver process is sufficient to ensure compliance with the law.

Regardless of whether the proposed waiver process is sufficient to ensure compliance with the law, hundreds of thousands of childhood CDRs still remain overdue. When CDRs are not conducted as scheduled, some recipients—regardless of age or impairment—may receive benefits for which they are no longer eligible. In September 2011, SSA's Office of the Inspector General estimated that SSA had paid about $1.4 billion in SSI benefits to approximately 513,000 recipients under age 18 who should have not received them—some of whom were pending reviews for 5 or more years.[74] They estimated that SSA will continue to make improper payments of approximately $461.6 million annually until these reviews are completed. Furthermore, in its most recently issued CDR report, SSA estimated a program savings of $9.30 for every $1 invested in conducting CDRs and projected that those CDRs conducted for adult SSDI and SSI recipients and for child SSI recipients combined in fiscal

---

[74]The SSA Inspector General estimated that SSA did not complete 79 percent of childhood CDRs and 10 percent of age 18 redeterminations on the basis of the results of 275 cases of physical and mental impairments they reviewed. To estimate the amount of SSI payments made because SSA had not completed a timely childhood CDR, the Inspector General calculated the amount of SSI payments made between the 1-year anniversary of the scheduled CDR date and the earlier of the month of cessation or April 2011 (the date the Inspector General reviewed the cases).

year 2010 would save federal programs the present value of estimated lifetime benefits of $3.5 billion.[75]

SSA and DDS officials have acknowledged that the agency has not conducted reviews for child recipients in a timely manner, and in some cases, they have not conducted childhood CDRs prior to a child's age 18 redetermination. One of the major objectives in SSA's newly issued Strategic Plan[76] is to "increase efforts to accurately pay benefits" and the Plan indicates that SSA intends to conduct more CDRs, as funding is available. Congressional appropriations for CDRs overall increased from $504 million in fiscal year 2009 to $758 million in fiscal year 2010 and have essentially remained at this level since that time, according to agency officials.[77] SSA continues to evaluate how to use this funding; however, it is not yet known to what extent the agency would increase the number of childhood CDRs in the future or target such CDRs toward those children with mental impairments who are likely to medically improve.

Conclusions

Children with mental impairments represent a growing number of applicants and recipients within the SSI program, which have contributed to the program's overall growth in recent years. However, a lack of key information about these children may present SSA with ongoing management challenges. In particular, the agency has taken steps to better understand program trends, but it does not comprehensively determine how multiple impairments influence eligibility decisions, in part

---

[75]This represents the combined savings to the SSI, SSDI, Medicare, and Medicaid programs from CDRs conducted for the SSI and Disability Insurance programs, from cessations and terminations due to failure to cooperate with a CDR in fiscal year 2010. The estimate includes savings to Medicare and Medicaid, as in some cases eligibility for SSI and SSDI confers eligibility for certain Medicare or Medicaid benefits, as well. SSA noted that the savings-to-cost ratio for fiscal year 2010 represents a significant drop from the average ratio for fiscal years 1996 through 2009 of $10.60 to $1, attributing the drop largely to the Medicaid estimates, which now reflect the effects of a Patient Protection and Affordable Care Act provision that allows most disabled SSI recipients terminated due to a CDR to retain their Medicaid coverage beginning January 1, 2014. *Annual Report of Continuing Disability Reviews, Fiscal Year 2010*, pp. 5, B-1, B-2.

[76]SSA, *Strategic Plan: Security Value for America, Fiscal Years 2013-2016* (Feb. 2012).

[77]Funding for CDRs in both fiscal years 2011 and 2012 was $756 million. The administration's fiscal year 2013 budget proposal includes a supplemental request of $140 million for CDRs and other program integrity activities for fiscal year 2012.

because DDS offices have not consistently collected secondary impairment data. Without steps to ensure that this information is more reliably recorded, SSA management will not have a complete picture of the characteristics of children with mental impairments receiving benefits or changes in this population over time.

Because examiners sometimes lack key information for cases they review, including school records and information on multiple children receiving benefits in the same household, they may face challenges in making eligibility decisions and identifying potential fraud or abuse. Examiners have also increasingly based allowance decisions on a finding of functional equivalence for children with the most prevalent mental impairments, requiring more complex decision making. Yet because some examiners face obstacles in obtaining information from schools—which they consider critical to understanding how a child functions—SSA cannot ensure that examiners have the necessary information to arrive at the most accurate determinations. Additionally, as a key program gatekeeper, DDS examiners are in a unique position to identify program integrity threats related to multiple children receiving SSI benefits within the same household. However, without better information on these types of arrangements they are unable fulfill this role in preventing potential fraud and abuse.

The fact that more than 430,000 childhood CDRs are overdue raises concerns about the agency's ability to manage limited funds in a manner that adequately balances its public service priorities with its stewardship responsibility. When reviews are not conducted as scheduled, some child recipients may receive benefits for which they are no longer eligible, potentially costing taxpayers billions of dollars in overpayments. Furthermore, CDRs provide an important check on program growth by removing ineligible recipients from the rolls, even while new applicants are added. If these reviews are not conducted in sufficient numbers, the agency will continue to struggle to contain growth in benefit payments, placing added burden on already strained federal budgets. Congress appropriated funding for SSA to conduct more CDRs in recent years, and SSA is evaluating how to manage its overall CDR workload. However, because SSA considers SSI childhood CDRs a lower priority than other CDRs, it is unclear whether the agency will use this funding to review children most likely to medically improve—reviews that could yield a high return on investment. If SSA continues to rely heavily on the use of waivers to conduct fewer CDRs than would otherwise be required by law, SSA will potentially forgo future program savings. Furthermore, while we consider SSA's decision to begin issuing formal waivers in order to clearly comply with the CDR legal requirement to be a good start, that action alone is not sufficient to fully alleviate our concerns with the waiver process. Until the agency formally implements this waiver process, the extent to which SSA is conducting CDRs consistently with its legal requirements will continue to be unclear.

Recommendations for Executive Action

To strengthen eligibility decisions and improve monitoring of children with mental impairments within the SSI program, we recommend that the Commissioner of Social Security:

1. Direct the Deputy Commissioners of Retirement and Disability Policy and Operations to take steps to ensure that DDS examiners accurately record information on secondary impairments in order to improve SSA's understanding of how multiple impairments may influence decisions.

2. Direct the Deputy Commissioner of Operations to identify the extent to which DDS examiners nationwide experience obstacles in obtaining teacher assessments and school records. To the extent these are identified, SSA should clarify the nature of these obstacles and formulate steps to address them. Such steps could include increased DDS outreach to primary and secondary schools, increased SSA coordination with the Department of Education, or additional guidance to DDS offices.

3. Direct the Deputy Commissioner of Operations to ensure that field offices notify their respective DDS offices of those claims in which multiple children within the same household are applying for or receiving SSI benefits so that examiners will be better able to identify potential fraud or abuse in the program and elevate these cases to the attention of SSA's fraud investigations unit.

4. Direct the Deputy Commissioner of Quality Performance to eliminate the existing CDR backlog of cases for children with impairments who are likely to improve and, on an ongoing basis, conduct CDRs at least every 3 years for all children with impairments who are likely to improve, as resources are made available for these purposes.

5. Direct the Deputy Commissioner of Quality Performance and Deputy Commissioner of Operations to take actions to ensure that SSA's CDR waiver process is open, transparent, and public. This may include promulgating formal guidance for issuing waivers, and a

process for making information about issued waivers available to the public.

Agency Comments and Our Evaluation

We provided a draft of this report to SSA for review and comment. In its written comments, reproduced in appendix V, SSA agreed with 4 of our 5 recommendations and stated that our draft report overall reflected a good understanding of the disability determination process and the SSI childhood disability program. SSA disagreed with our recommendation to eliminate the existing CDR backlog of cases for children with impairments who are likely to improve and conduct CDRs for these children at least every 3 years, as resources are made available for these purposes. SSA agreed conceptually that it should complete more CDRs for SSI children but emphasized that it is constrained by limited funding and staff resources and as a result had to waive many required childhood CDRs in recent years. SSA also argued that performing additional SSI child CDRs would have negative impacts on the SSDI program. We acknowledge the challenge SSA faces as it strives to balance competing workloads. In recognition of the agency's resource constraints, we noted in our recommendation that additional CDRs for children who are likely to medically improve should be conducted "as resources are made available for these purposes." We also believe that the increased appropriations for CDRs in recent years provides SSA with added flexibility for balancing these competing workloads. Moreover, it is important to recognize we are not recommending that SSA eliminate its ongoing SSDI CDR efforts. Rather, we believe that more attention is needed for SSI children's cases to address the existing backlog, especially given the relatively few CDRs conducted in this area in recent years, and the high average cessation rate for these cases. SSA also provided technical comments that we have incorporated, as appropriate.

We are sending copies of this report to the Commissioner of Social Security, appropriate congressional committees, and other interested parties. In addition, the report is available at no charge on the GAO website at http://www.gao.gov.

If you or your staff have any questions about this report, please contact me at (202) 512-7215 or bertonid@gao.gov. Contact points for our Offices of Congressional Relations and Public Affairs may be found on the last page of this report. GAO staff who made major contributions to this report are listed in appendix VI.

Daniel Bertoni
Director
Education, Workforce,
   and Income Security Issues

Appendix I: Scope and Methodology

Our review focused on (1) the trends in the rate of children receiving Supplemental Security Income (SSI) benefits due to mental impairments; (2) the role that medical and nonmedical information, such as medication and school records, play in the initial determination of a child's medical eligibility; and (3) the steps the Social Security Administration (SSA) has taken to monitor the continued medical eligibility of these children.

To examine these issues, we analyzed SSA data on (1) the overall number of initial disability determinations and allowances, (2) annual benefit awards and recipients, (3) the number and types of mental impairments, (4) the number of children receiving SSI benefits residing in households where other children also receive SSI benefits, and (5) the number of continuing disability reviews of children conducted by SSA. In reviewing these data, we acknowledge that the child population in the United States has also grown since 2000 and demographics of this population may have changed since that time. We assessed the reliability of the data presented in this report by performing data testing, reviewing internal controls and related documentation, and interviewing agency officials, and found potential limitations with the extent to which primary and secondary impairment coding within SSA's 831 Disability file—the file that contains data on disability determinations—may be complete. However, because the 831 Disability file is used by SSA to make, and thus reflect, the decisions made regarding medical determinations, we determined that these data were sufficiently reliable to describe certain trends among children in the SSI program.

We also conducted in-depth interviews with SSA management and line staff at SSA headquarters and within six SSA regions—Atlanta, Georgia; Dallas, Texas; Chicago, Illinois; Philadelphia, Pennsylvania; Boston, Massachusetts; and San Francisco, California. Our work included site visits to 9 field offices within these regions, as well as 11 state disability determination services (DDS) offices (state agencies under the direction of SSA that perform medical eligibility determinations and continuing disability reviews of SSI applicants). We performed separate interviews with SSA field office district managers, supervisors, and claims representatives, and with DDS managers, supervisors, examiners, and medical or psychological consultants, when they were available. We selected these sites on the basis of their geographic location, high volume of SSI applications for children with mental impairments, and variety of benefit allowance rates for children with mental impairments. In addition, we interviewed numerous external experts from the medical and disability advocacy communities and reviewed relevant studies to identify factors that may be currently affecting the growth and composition of the childhood disability applicants and recipients, especially for those children with mental impairments. However, the relative effects of any potential factors we identified on the SSI program's growth are not fully known and were beyond the scope of this report. We also reviewed relevant federal laws and regulations.

We conducted a case file review to verify information obtained through our interviews with DDS office staff and to better understand the role of secondary impairments in determinations as well as what information examiners use when determining a child's medical eligibility. We reviewed a probability sample of 298 case files selected from the 184,150 initial determinations decided in fiscal year 2010 for children with alleged attention deficit hyperactivity disorder (ADHD),[1] speech and language delay, and autistic disorder and other pervasive development disorders (autism).[2] (Through the initial determination process, the DDS assesses whether the child's impairment can be established through medical evidence—not only by the individual's statement of symptoms—as well as the severity of the impairment and whether the impairment results in marked and severe functional limitations.) We reviewed electronic case files for children with mental impairments and SSA forms to develop a standardized data collection instrument. We completed a data collection instrument for each initial determination in our sample, and each record was independently reviewed by another staff person for clarity and accuracy. We based our observations of the sources examiners used to support their determinations on examiners' remarks in the Childhood Disability Evaluation Form (form SSA-538-F6) and the Disability Determination Explanation. Because our purpose was not to assess the appropriateness of examiners' decisions but to understand what information sources examiners used in explaining the rationale for their decision-making, we did not attempt to adjudicate these cases ourselves. Our observations were limited by the extent to which examiners documented their analysis and rationale on these forms. We found the examiners' remarks sufficient to characterize which sources were used to support decisions, but examiners provided varying levels of detail in their

---

[1]Children with attention deficit disorder are also included in this category.

[2]We originally sampled 300 cases for review but encountered 2 cases that were either mis-coded or that lacked an electronic case file. We excluded these 2 cases from our analysis, which produced an effective sample size of 298.

remarks and we had no basis for judging whether additional sources of information were used to support but were not reported.

As with all probability samples, estimates from our case file review are subject to sampling errors. Sampling errors occur because we use a sample to draw conclusions about a larger population. If a different sample had been taken, the results might have been different. To recognize the possibility that other samples might have yielded other results, we express our confidence in the precision of our particular sample's results as a 95 percent confidence interval. The 95 percent confidence interval is expected to include the population value for 95 percent of samples of this type. When we make estimates for this population, we are 95 percent confident that the results we obtained are within plus or minus 8 percentage points of what we would have obtained if we had included the entire population within our review, unless otherwise noted. The text of our report provides more specific confidence intervals for various estimates.

We selected the sample from within six strata, consisting of allowance and denial decisions and the three most prevalent primary impairments among medical allowances for children with mental impairments—ADHD, speech and language delay, and autism. We sampled approximately the same number of cases from each stratum in order to ensure that the sample sizes were sufficient to produce precise estimates within each combination of impairment and decision. When generalizing to the overall population and to various subpopulations, we weighted each case according to its probability of selection, which varied across strata due to differences in the number of cases in the stratum populations.

We conducted this performance audit from February 2011 to June 2012 in accordance with generally accepted government auditing standards. Those standards require that we plan and perform the audit to obtain sufficient, appropriate evidence to provide a reasonable basis for our findings and conclusions based on our audit objectives. We believe the evidence obtained provides a reasonable basis for findings and conclusions based on our audit objectives.

Appendix II: Listings for Mental Disorders for Children under Age 18

The structure of the mental disorders listings for children under age 18 parallels the structure for the mental disorders listings for adults but is modified to reflect the presentation of mental disorders in children. Under federal regulations, when a child is not performing substantial gainful activity and the impairment is severe, the Social Security Administration (SSA) will examine whether the child's impairment meets, medically equals, or functionally equals any of the impairments contained in the listings. The listings further describe the level of severity necessary to meet these requirements. The listings for mental disorders in children are grouped into 11 diagnostic categories:[1]

Organic mental disorders. Abnormalities in perception, cognition, affect, or behavior associated with dysfunction of the brain. The history and physical examination or laboratory tests, including psychological or neuropsychological tests, demonstrate or support the presence of an organic factor judged to be etiologically related to the abnormal mental state and associated deficit or loss of specific cognitive abilities, or affective changes, or loss of previously acquired functional abilities.

Schizophrenic, delusional (paranoid), schizoaffective, and other psychotic disorders. Onset of psychotic features, characterized by a marked disturbance of thinking, feeling, and behavior, with deterioration from a previous level of functioning or failure to achieve the expected level of social functioning.

Mood disorders. Characterized by a disturbance of mood (referring to a prolonged emotion that colors the whole psychic life, generally involving either depression or elation), accompanied by a full or partial manic or depressive syndrome.

Mental retardation. Characterized by significantly sub-average general intellectual functioning with deficits in adaptive functioning.[2]

---

[1]For purposes of this appendix, we have provided basic information about the 11 mental disorders for children included in SSA's listings. For additional information about these listings, refer to 20 C.F.R. pt. 404, subpt. P, app. 1.

[2]Although for most purposes SSA refers to intellectual disabilities rather than mental retardation, consistent with Rosa's Law, its medical listings have not been updated to reflect this change.

Anxiety disorders. In these disorders, anxiety is either the predominant disturbance or is experienced if the individual attempts to master symptoms; for example, confronting the dreaded object or situation in a phobic disorder, attempting to go to school in a separation anxiety disorder, resisting the obsessions or compulsions in an obsessive compulsive disorder, or confronting strangers or peers in avoidant disorders.

Somatoform, eating, and tic disorders. Manifested by physical symptoms for which there are no demonstrable organic findings or known physiologic mechanisms; or eating or tic disorders with physical manifestations.

Personality disorders. Manifested by pervasive, inflexible, and maladaptive personality traits, which are typical of the child's long-term functioning and not limited to discrete episodes of illness.

Psychoactive substance dependence disorders. Manifested by a cluster of cognitive, behavioral, and physiologic symptoms that indicate impaired control of psychoactive substance use with continued use of the substance despite adverse consequences.

Autistic disorder and other pervasive developmental disorders. Characterized by qualitative deficits in the development of reciprocal social interaction, in the development of verbal and nonverbal communication skills, and in imaginative activity. Often, there is a markedly restricted repertoire of activities and interests, which frequently are stereotyped and repetitive.

Attention deficit hyperactivity disorder. Manifested by developmentally inappropriate degrees of inattention, impulsiveness, and hyperactivity.

Developmental and emotional disorders of newborn and younger infants (birth to attainment of age 1): Developmental or emotional disorders of infancy are evidenced by a deficit or lag in the areas of motor, cognitive/communicative, or social functioning. These disorders may be related either to organic or to functional factors or to a combination of these factors.

According to SSA, these listings are examples of common mental disorders that are severe enough to result in a child being disabled. When a child has a medically determinable impairment that is not listed, an impairment that does not meet the requirements of a listing, or a combination of impairments in which none meets the requirements of a listing, SSA will make a determination whether the child's impairment or impairments medically or functionally equal the listings.[3] This can be especially important in older infants and toddlers (age 1 to attainment of age 3), who may be too young for identification of a specific diagnosis, yet demonstrate serious functional limitations. Therefore, the determination of equivalency is necessary to the evaluation of any child's case when the child does not have an impairment that meets a listing.

[3]See 20 C.F.R. §§ 416.926 and 416.926a.

Appendix III: Trends on the Three Most Prevalent Primary Impairments among Children with Mental Impairments in the Supplemental Security Income Program

Social Security Administration (SSA) data show that the three most prevalent primary mental impairments among those children allowed for Supplemental Security Income (SSI) benefits in fiscal year 2011 were for (1) attention deficit disorder or attention deficit hyperactivity disorder (ADHD),[1] (2) speech and language delay, and (3) autistic disorder and other pervasive development disorders (autism). These data are based on the primary impairment as designated by the disability determination services (DDS) examiner.[2] SSA's policy operations manual directs DDS examiners to code the primary impairment as the most severe condition that rendered the child disabled. However, SSA officials have acknowledged that primary impairment codes are sometimes missing or inaccurately coded.[3]

The following information provides a brief summary of each of these three primary impairments as they compare to the incidence of all mental impairments, as well as in terms of the proportion of applications, allowances, and receipts. Data represented as "applications" reflect SSI benefit claims where a DDS examiner made an initial disability determination decision. Some applications may have been submitted prior to the year when a determination was made. In addition, some applications could have more than one determination if the claim is selected for a quality review or if the disability claim is updated during the same year.

ADHD. From fiscal years 2000 to 2011, applications for this condition as a primary impairment more than doubled, from about 55,204 to 124,217, while allowances have also doubled from 13,857 to 29,872 (see fig. 10). By December 2011, almost 221,000 such children were receiving SSI benefits, and they comprised 26 percent of child recipients with mental impairments on the rolls.

---

[1] Children with attention deficit disorder are included in the ADHD category.

[2] The recorded primary impairment code identifies the primary impairment used in the medical determination for an individual's eligibility for SSI disability benefits. It appears in the SSA's 831 and 832/833 Disability files.

[3] According to SSA officials, the error rate for impairment coding is estimated between 5 and 6 percent.

GAO-12-497 Supplemental Security Income

Appendix III: Trends on the Three Most
Prevalent Primary Impairments among
Children with Mental Impairments in the
Supplemental Security Income Program

Figure 10: Applications for Children with ADHD as a Primary Impairment, Fiscal Years 2000 to 2011

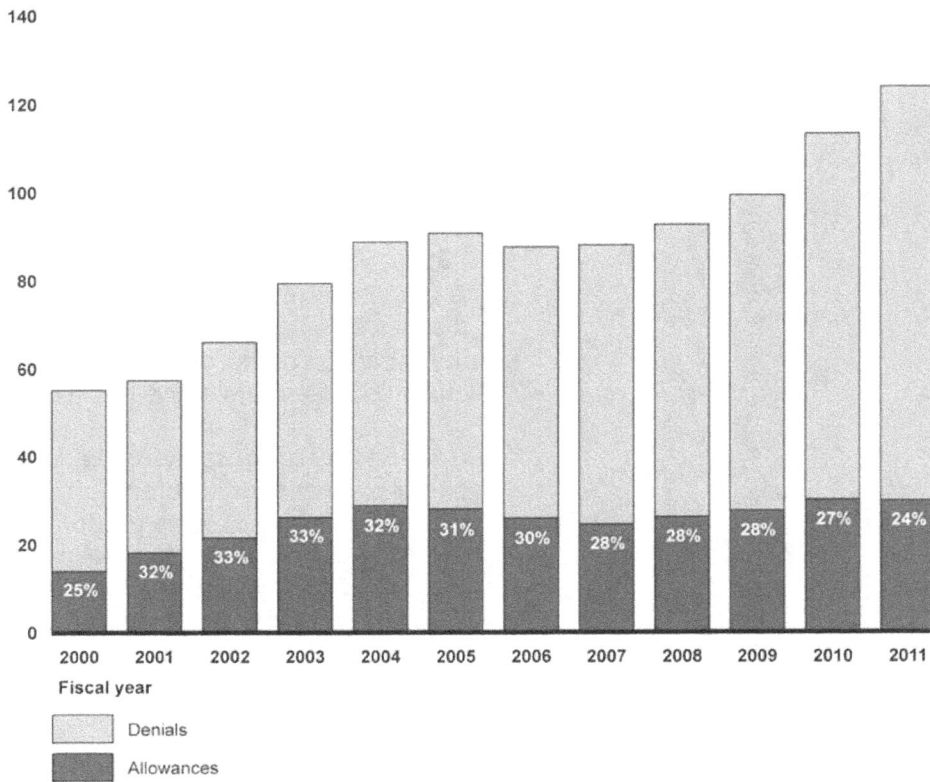

Source: GAO analysis of SSA data from the 831 Disability file.

Note: The information highlighted in this graphic is based on the primary impairment code recorded in the disability determination. Data represented as "applications" reflect SSI benefit claims where an initial disability determination decision was made. Some applications may have been submitted prior to the year when a determination was made. In addition, some applications could have more than one determination decision if selected for a quality review or if the disability claim is updated during the same year. Such determinations are reflected in the data presented in the figure.

While children with ADHD represent the single largest primary diagnostic group, SSA has denied the majority of ADHD child applicants since fiscal year 2000, because they were not medically eligible. Some DDS examiners we interviewed said that they rarely find a child medically eligible for benefits solely on the basis of a ADHD impairment alone, but

Appendix III: Trends on the Three Most
Prevalent Primary Impairments among
Children with Mental Impairments in the
Supplemental Security Income Program

more commonly in combination with another impairment, such as oppositional defiant disorder. In our case file review, we found 37 of 50 ADHD allowances had a secondary impairment present,[4] and oppositional defiant disorder was the secondary impairment cited most frequently in the individual cases we reviewed.

SSA officials suggested that the increase in both applications and allowances for children with ADHD might be attributable to an increase in diagnoses over the last decade, and cited a National Institute of Health survey finding that ADHD diagnoses had increased by 3 percent, on average, from 1996 to 2006 and by 5.5 percent, on average, from 2003 to 2007.[5] SSA officials also noted a 2008 medical study reporting that ADHD is one of the most commonly diagnosed childhood neurobehavioral disorders.[6] In addition, the National Institute of Mental Health has stated that attention deficit disorder and ADHD are among the most common childhood disorders in the United States.

Speech and language delays. Since fiscal year 2000, both applications and allowances for children with speech and language delays have increased overall, but the proportion of applicants found medically eligible has ranged from 54 to 61 percent during this period. From fiscal year 2000 to 2011, applications for this impairment more than doubled, from 21,615 to 51,740 while the number of children allowed increased from 11,565 to 29,309 (see fig. 11).

[4]We reviewed a probability sample of 298 case files selected from the 184,150 initial determinations decided in fiscal year 2010 for children with alleged ADHD, speech and language delay, and autism.

[5]Centers for Disease Control and Prevention/National Survey of Children's Health, National Health Interview Survey, 2004-2006.

[6]P.N. Pastor and C.A. Reuben, Diagnosed attention deficit hyperactivity disorder and learning disability: United States, 2004-2006. Vital Health Stat 2008; 10 (237).

Appendix III: Trends on the Three Most
Prevalent Primary Impairments among
Children with Mental Impairments in the
Supplemental Security Income Program

**Figure 11: Applications for Children with Speech and Language Delays as a Primary
Impairment, Fiscal Years 2000 to 2011**

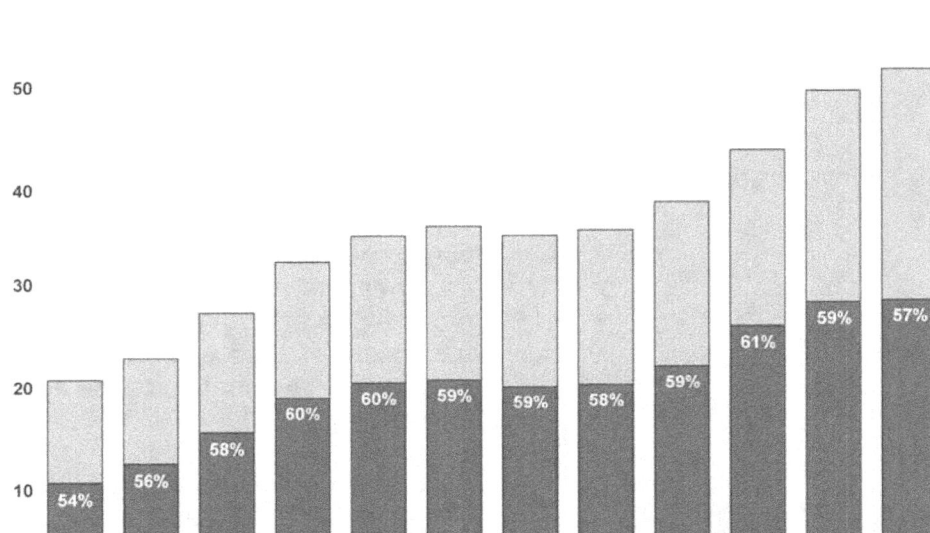

Source: GAO analysis of SSA data from the 831 Disability file.

Note: The information highlighted in this graphic is based on the primary impairment code recorded in
the disability determination. Data represented as "applications" reflect SSI benefit claims where an
initial disability determination decision was made. Some applications may have been submitted prior
to the year when a determination was made. In addition, some applications may have been submitted
could have more than one determination decision if selected for a quality review or if the disability
claim is updated during the same year. Such determinations are reflected in the data in the figure.

Some DDS officials we interviewed attributed the increased number of
children applying for and receiving SSI benefits to speech and language
delay to increased school testing and screening program services offered
under the Individuals with Disabilities Education Act (IDEA). The U.S.
Department of Education noted in their latest annual report that teachers
indicated that 89 percent of the children aged 3 through 5 years served
under IDEA received speech or language therapy in the 2003 to 2004
school year, and 86 percent received it in the 2004 to 2005 school year,

GAO-12-497 Supplemental Security Income

Appendix III: Trends on the Three Most
Prevalent Primary Impairments among
Children with Mental Impairments in the
Supplemental Security Income Program

making it the most common service in both years.[7] In addition, they noted that speech and language impairments were one of the most common disability categories among students aged 6 through 21 years served under IDEA, Part B, in the fall of 2006. Of these more than 6 million students aged 6 through 21 years, about 1.2 million, or 19.1 percent, received services due to a speech and language impairment.

Some speech and language experts from across the United States told us that they were surprised by the increased number of children receiving SSI benefits, but acknowledged that the definitions of disability for IDEA and the SSI program are different. They added that in some instances speech and language disorder may be a provisional diagnosis for very young children when it may be difficult to pinpoint a specific impairment or impairments, which they believed could be contributing to program growth. SSA officials told us that further study was needed to better understand increases of this impairment. As of February 2012, SSA was considering whether to propose new rules for evaluating language and speech and disorders.[8]

Autism. From fiscal year 2000 to 2011, autism applications increased by almost 400 percent from 5,430 to 26,739, and allowances increased similarly from 5,050 to 22,931 (see fig.12). As of December 2011, about 107,000 (12 percent) children with mental impairments were receiving SSI benefits due to autistic disorders. From fiscal year 2000 to 2011, DDS examiners found from 86 to 94 percent of those children applying for SSI on the basis of autism medically eligible for benefits.

---

[7]U.S. Department of Education, Office of Special Education and Rehabilitative Services. Office of Special Education Programs, *30th Annual Report to Congress on the Implementation of the Individuals with Disabilities Education Act, 2008* (Washington, D.C.: December 2011).

[8]The new rules would apply to disability claims involving language and speech disorders in adults and children under tiltes II and XVI of the Social Security Act. Specifically, SSA was considering whether to add a new body system in the Listing of Impairments in appendix 1 to subpart P of part 404 of its regulations (listings) for these disorders.

Appendix III: Trends on the Three Most
Prevalent Primary Impairments among
Children with Mental Impairments in the
Supplemental Security Income Program

Figure 12: Applications for Children with Autism as a Primary Impairment, Fiscal Years 2000 to 2011

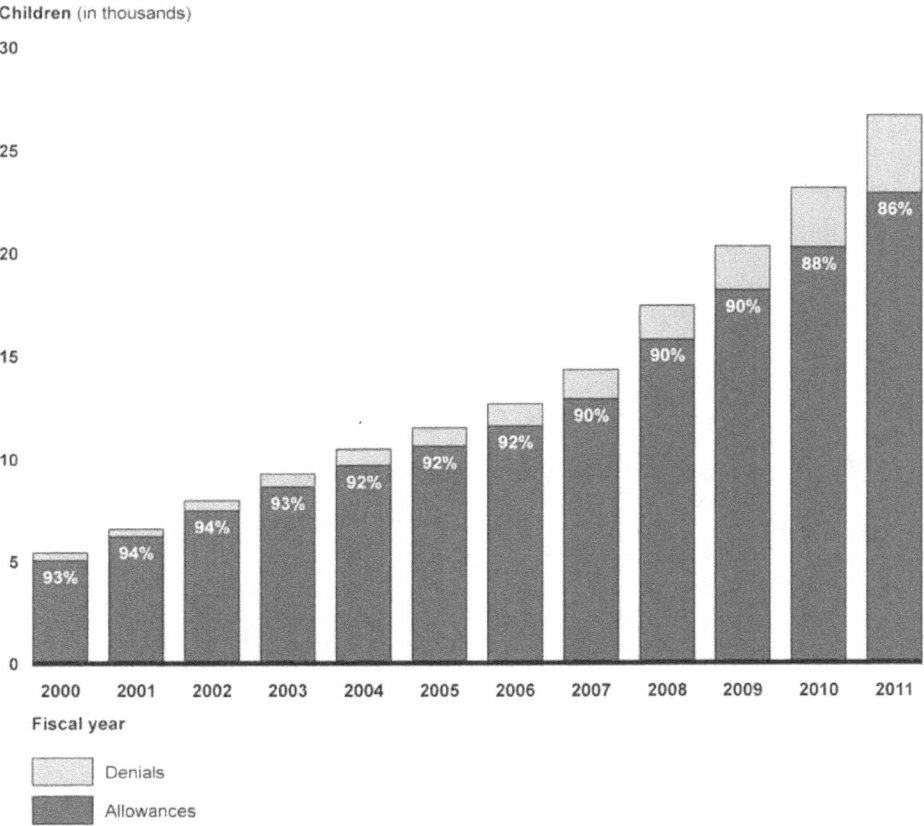

Children (in thousands)

Fiscal year

☐ Denials

■ Allowances

Source: GAO analysis of SSA data from the 831 Disability file.

Note: The information highlighted in this graphic is based on the primary impairment code recorded in the disability determination. Data represented as "applications" reflect SSI benefit claims where an initial disability determination decision was made. Some applications may have been submitted prior to the year when a determination was made. In addition, some applications could have more than one determination decision if selected for a quality review or if the disability claim is updated during the same year. Such determinations are reflected in the data presented in the figure.

SSA officials primarily attribute the increase in the number of autism applications and allowances over the years to greater incidences of autism among children and explained that some children who may have previously been diagnosed as intellectually disabled are instead being diagnosed as autistic. In fact, the number of children applying for and receiving SSI benefits due to "intellectual disability" or "mental retardation" has significantly declined since fiscal year 2000. Children receiving benefits due to an intellectual disability comprised 51 percent of all mental

Appendix III: Trends on the Three Most
Prevalent Primary Impairments among
Children with Mental Impairments in the
Supplemental Security Income Program

claims in fiscal year 2000 and 15 percent in fiscal year 2011. According to
one study SSA cited, the prevalence of autism in children has increased
by 2.5 percent, from 0.6 per 1,000 live births in 1994 to 3.1 per 1,000 live
births in 2003, while during the same period, the prevalence of mental
retardation and learning disabilities declined by 2.8 and 8.3 per 1,000,
respectively.[9] In addition, the Centers for Disease Controls and
Prevention estimated in March 2012 that on average 1 in 88 children in
the United States has an autism spectrum disorder, but the extent to
which this reflects increases in awareness and access to services or
actual increases in the prevalence of autism symptoms is not known.

On the basis of our case file review, we also identified some
characteristics of children for whom SSA made an initial determination in
fiscal year 2010 for ADHD, speech and language delay, and autism. For
example, as shown in figure 13, more than 60 percent of these children
had ADHD.

Figure 13: Number of Fiscal Year 2010 Initial Determinations for Children, by
Primary Impairment

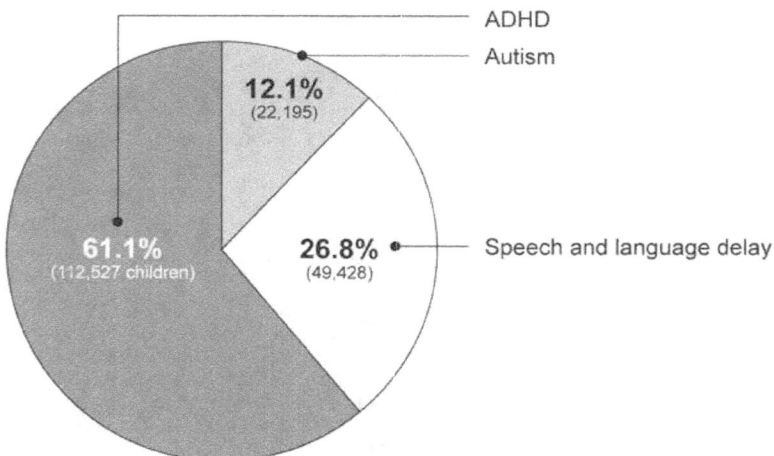

ADHD

Autism

12.1%
(22,195)

61.1%
(112,527 children)

26.8%
(49,428)

Speech and language delay

Source: GAO analysis of SSA 831 Disability file data on all fiscal year 2010 initial determinations for children with alleged ADHD,
speech and language delay, and autism.

[9]P.T. Shattuck, "The Contribution of Diagnostic Substitution to the Growing Administrative
Prevalence of Autism in the U.S. Special Education Data." *Pediatrics*, vol. 117, no. 4 (Apr.
1, 2006) 1028-1037.

Appendix III: Trends on the Three Most
Prevalent Primary Impairments among
Children with Mental Impairments in the
Supplemental Security Income Program

The age at which SSA determined whether a child was medically eligible for benefits varied by impairment (see fig. 14). Children with ADHD who applied for benefits were older, on average, than applicants with autism or speech and language delay.

Appendix III: Trends on the Three Most
Prevalent Primary Impairments among
Children with Mental Impairments in the
Supplemental Security Income Program

Figure 14: Number of Fiscal Year 2010 Initial Determinations for Children, by Primary Impairment and Age

ADHD
112,527
total cases

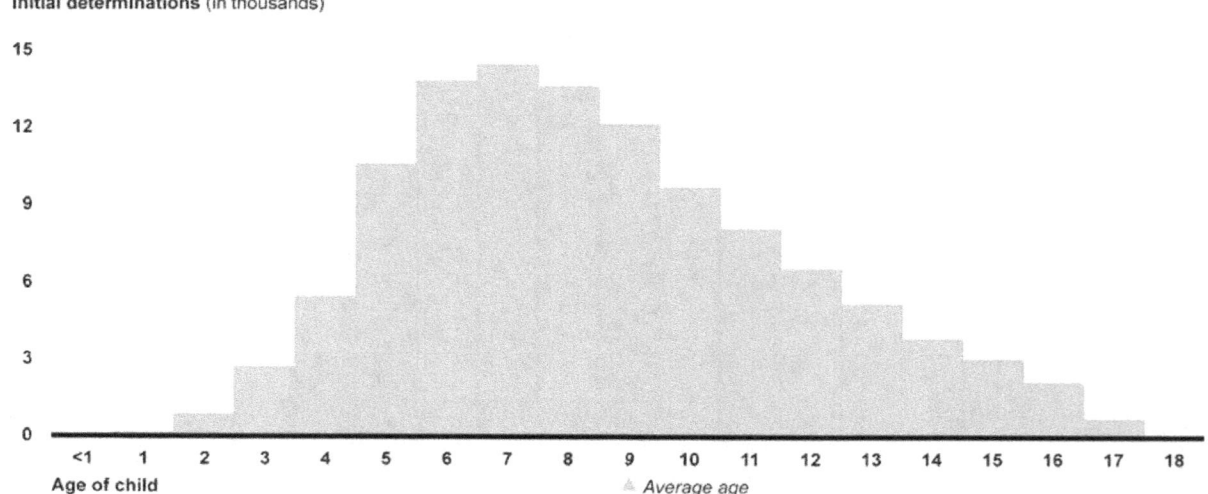

**Speech
and
language
delay**
49,428
total cases

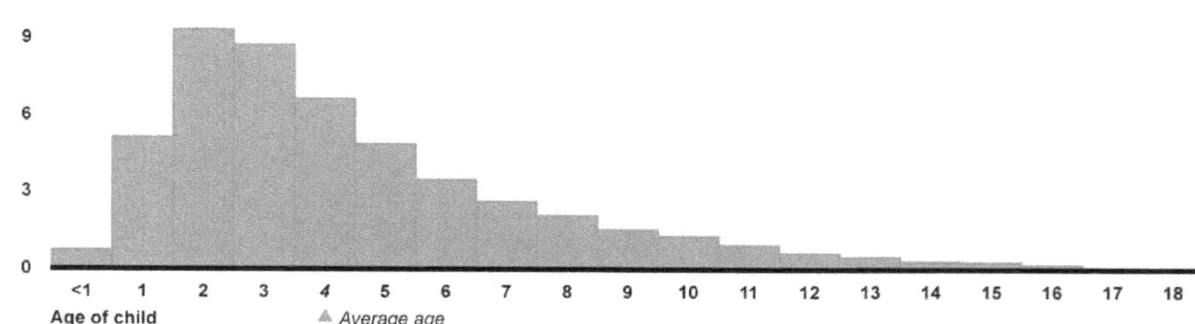

Autism
22,195
total cases

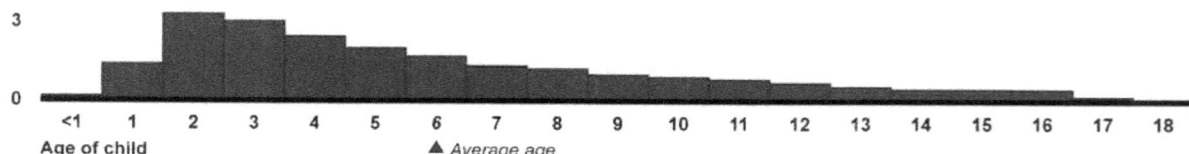

Source: GAO analysis of SSA 831 Disability file data on all fiscal year 2010 initial determinations for children with alleged ADHD, speech and language delay, and autism.

Note: Age is calculated as of the beginning of fiscal year 2010.

Appendix III: Trends on the Three Most
Prevalent Primary Impairments among
Children with Mental Impairments in the
Supplemental Security Income Program

Based on our case file review, we estimate that 72 percent of these
children were male, although gender composition also varied by
impairment (see fig. 15). As discussed in appendix I of this report, we
reviewed case files from a stratified probability sample of determinations
made in fiscal year 2010.

**Figure 15: Percentage of Fiscal Year 2010 Initial Determinations for Children, by
Primary Impairment and Gender**

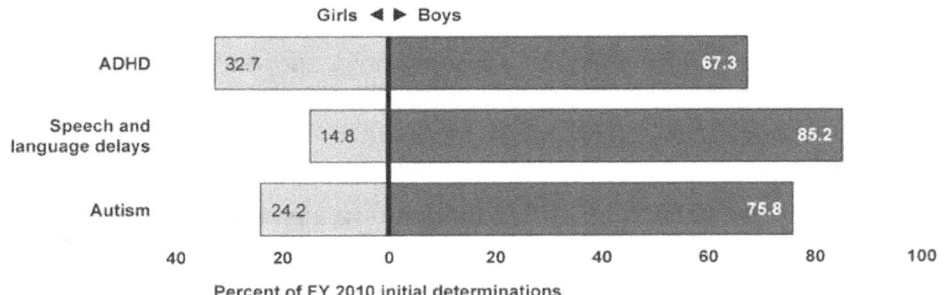

Source: GAO estimates based on case file review of sampled fiscal year 2010 initial determinations for children with alleged ADHD,
speech and language delay, and autism.

Note: The 95 percent margin of error for each estimate does not exceed plus or minus 10 percentage
points.

Appendix IV: Reported Medication and Psychotropic Drug Use among Children Applying for Supplemental Security Income by Select Impairments, Fiscal Year 2010

In our review of a generalizable probability sample of 298 initial determinations performed in fiscal year 2010 for children with alleged attention deficit hyperactivity disorder (ADHD),[1] speech and language delay, and autistic disorder and other pervasive development disorders (autism), we found parents reported that their children were prescribed some form of medication in 58 percent of these cases. More specifically, parents reported that their children were prescribed psychotropic drugs in 47 percent of these cases (see table 1). Children with ADHD accounted for the vast majority of those reportedly using medication or psychotropic drugs—79 percent and 90 percent, respectively (see table 2). The most commonly reported psychotropic drugs were Concerta, Ritalin, and Adderall, which are prescribed to treat ADHD, as well as Risperdal, which is an antipsychotic. Of children reportedly prescribed psychotropic drugs, the majority reported using one psychotropic drug.

Table 1: Percentage of Cases by Reported Use of Medication and by Select Primary Impairment, Fiscal Year 2010

	Primary impairment			
	ADHD	Autism	Speech and language delay	Total
Medication reported	45.9%	3.5%	8.5%	**58.0%**
	(5.9)	(1.3)	(2.5)	**(6.5)**
Medication not reported	15.2	8.6	18.3	**42.0%**
	(5.9)	(1.3)	(2.5)	**(6.5)**
Psychotropic drugs reported	42.3	2.2	2.4	**46.9%**
	(6.3)	(1.1)	(1.5)	**(6.5)**
Psychotropic drugs not reported	18.8	9.9	24.4	**53.1%**
	(6.3)	(1.1)	(1.5)	**(6.5)**

Source: GAO analysis of Social Security Administration 831 Disability file data on all fiscal year 2010 initial determinations for children with ADHD, speech and language delay, and autism.

Note: Entries in parentheses are 95 percent margins of error.

---

[1]Children with attention deficit disorder are also included in this category.

Table 2: Percentage of Medication and Psychotropic Drug Use Reported by Select Primary Impairment, Fiscal Year 2010

Primary impairment	Medication reported	Medication not reported	Psychotropic drugs reported	Psychotropic drugs not reported
ADHD	79.3%	36.1%	90.2%	35.4%
	(4.4)	(9.3)	(3.8)	(7.7)
Autism	6.0	20.4	4.6	18.6
	(2.3)	(4.0)	(2.4)	(2.8)
Speech and language delay	14.7	43.6	5.2	46.0
	(3.9)	(7.1)	(3.0)	(5.7)
Total	**100.0%**	**100.1%**	**100.0%**	**100.0%**

Source: GAO analysis of SSA 831 Disability file data on all fiscal year 2010 initial determinations for children with ADHD, speech and language delay, and autism.

Note: Some totals may not add to 100 percent due to rounding. Entries in parentheses are 95 percent margins of error.

Appendix V: Comments from the Social Security Administration

SOCIAL SECURITY
Office of the Commissioner

June 11, 2012

Mr. Daniel Bertoni, Director
Education, Workforce, and Income Security Issues
United States Government Accountability Office
441 G. Street, NW
Washington, D.C. 20548

Dear Mr. Bertoni,

Thank you for the opportunity to review the draft report, "SUPPLEMENTAL SECURITY INCOME: Better Management Oversight Needed for Children's Benefits" (GAO-12-497). Our response is enclosed.

If you have any questions, please contact me at (410) 965-0520. Your staff may contact Amy Thompson, Senior Advisor for Records Management and Audit Liaison Staff, at (410) 966-0569.

Sincerely,

Dean S. Landis
Deputy Chief of Staff

Enclosure

SOCIAL SECURITY ADMINISTRATION   BALTIMORE, MD 21235-0001

COMMENTS ON THE GOVERNMENT ACCOUNTABILITY OFFICE (GAO) DRAFT REPORT, "SUPPLEMENTAL SECURITY INCOME: BETTER MANAGEMENT OVERSIGHT NEEDED FOR CHILDREN'S BENEFITS" (GAO-12-497)

GENERAL COMMENTS

It appears the auditors examined Supplemental Security Income (SSI) childhood disability payments as an independently funded workload, which it is not. Our other important and mandatory program integrity work competes for the same scarce resources as SSI childhood payments. While we agree conceptually that we should complete more continuing disability reviews (CDR) on SSI childhood payments, our ability to do so is limited by the funding we receive from Congress. Based on Congress' decision to commit insufficient resources for the goals it authorizes and requires, we prioritize the program integrity work that produces the best return on investment.

We consider several factors when prioritizing CDRs. GAO's findings seem to focus on cessation rates as the primary factor in determining our return for completing CDRs. In fiscal year (FY) 2011, over 10 million Social Security Disability Insurance (SSDI) beneficiaries received $128 billion in benefits. Therefore, we conduct more SSDI CDRs because SSDI beneficiaries have benefit rates that are, on average, almost twice as much as SSI childhood payment rates and usually have longer payback periods in the savings calculations. Although we agree that the review of childhood cases would produce a higher percentage of cessations, the review of SSDI adult cases generally produces greater lifetime savings. If GAO disagrees with our approach, GAO should be transparent with Congress about the loss to the trust funds entailed by its approach.

Our overall program savings to administrative cost ratios support the fact that we responsibly use our limited resources in the most cost-effective manner. We began calculating savings ratios for the CDR Report to Congress in the late 1990s, and since FY 2006 the ratios have been about $10 to $1.

Overall, this draft report reflects a good understanding of our disability determination process and the SSI childhood disability program, but it does not acknowledge our repeated, but only partially successful, requests for additional funding to support completing additional CDRs. Despite operating for each of the last two years with less funding than we had in FY 2010, we have steadily increased the number of medical CDRs we complete. We have also increased the number of SSI childhood CDRs we complete each year. It is also important to understand that it is not just funding that affects our ability to complete this work. We must also have enough trained employees because the same people who handle our medical CDR work also make initial disability determinations, which have increased by about 30 percent since FY 2007.

2

RESPONSES TO THE RECOMMENDATIONS

Recommendation 1

Direct the Deputy Commissioners of Retirement and Disability Policy and Operations to take steps to ensure that DDS examiners accurately record information on secondary impairments in order to improve SSA's understanding of how multiple impairments may influence decisions.

Response

We agree.

Recommendation 2

Direct the Deputy Commissioner of Operations to identify the extent to which DDS examiners nationwide experience obstacles in obtaining teacher assessments and school records. To the extent these are identified, SSA should clarify the nature of these obstacles and formulate steps to address them. Such steps could include increased DDS outreach to primary and secondary schools, increased SSA coordination with the Department of Education, or additional guidance to DDS offices.

Response

We agree.

Recommendation 3

Direct the Deputy Commissioner of Operations to ensure that field offices notify their respective DDS offices of those claims in which multiple children within the same household are applying for or receiving SSI benefits so that examiners will be better able to identify potential fraud or abuse in the program and elevate these cases to the attention of SSA's fraud investigations unit.

Response

We agree. As resources allow, we will explore ways to modify our policy and systems to provide this notification.

Recommendation 4

Direct the Deputy Commissioner of Quality Performance to eliminate the existing CDR backlog of cases for children with impairments who are likely to improve and, on an ongoing basis, conduct CDRs at least every 3 years for all children with impairments who are likely to improve, as resources are made available for these purposes.

3

Response

We disagree. While we would like to conduct more program integrity reviews and meet the
CDR goals established by Congress, budget restrictions have forced us to waive many childhood
SSI CDRs in recent years. Given adequate funding, we would increase these reviews and target
cases that are most likely to show medical improvement, but it would mislead Congress to
suggest that this problem can be resolved by administrative fiat.

Recommendation 5

Direct the Deputy Commissioner of Quality Performance and Deputy Commissioner of
Operations to take actions to ensure that SSA's CDR waiver process is open, transparent, and
public. This may include promulgating formal guidance for issuing waivers, and a process for
making information about waivers available to the public.

Response

We agree. As stated in the April 20, 2012 letter to GAO from our Office of the General Counsel,
we are currently developing a more formal waiver process. However, we believe GAO should
make it clear to Congress that the statutory waiver scheme relies on assumptions about
predictable and adequate funding that have not been true for almost a decade, and that it would
be timely for Congress to revisit this statutory scheme.

Appendix VI: GAO Contact and Staff Acknowledgments

GAO Contact	Daniel Bertoni, (202) 512-7215 or bertonid@gao.gov
Staff Acknowledgments	In addition to the contact named above, Jeremy Cox (Assistant Director), James Bennett, Alexander Galuten, Jason Holsclaw, Kristen Jones, Sheila McCoy, Luann Moy, Ernest Powell, Jeff Tessin, and Paul Wright made key contributions to this report and the related e-supplement.